A GUIDE TO MAKING OPEN TEXTBOOKS WITH STUDENTS

A Guide to Making Open Textbooks with Students

Ed. Elizabeth Mays

Amanda Coolidge, Anna Andrzejewski, Apurva Ashok, Assistant Editors Zoe Wake Hyde, David Squires, Gabriel Higginbotham, Interviews with Alice Barrett, Julie Ward, Matthew Moore, Maxwell Nicholson, Rajiv Jhangiani, Robin DeRosa, Samara Burns, Steel Wagstaff, and Timothy Robbins

The Rebus Community for Open Textbook Creation

Montreal

A Guide to Making Open Textbooks with Students by Rebus Community is licensed under a Creative Commons Attribution 4.0 International License, except where otherwise noted.

©Elizabeth Mays, Robin DeRosa, Rajiv Jhangiani, Timothy Robbins, David Squires, Julie Ward, Anna Andrzejewski, Samara Burns, Matthew Moore. Interviews with Alice Barrett, Amanda Coolidge, Maxwell Nicholson, Steel Wagstaff, and Gabriel Higginbotham. All authors retain the copyright on their work.

Except where otherwise noted, all work in this book is licensed under a Creative Commons Attribution license (CC BY 4.0), meaning you can use it, adapt it, and redistribute it as you like, but you must provide attribution to the original authors, by retaining this license notice.

We request that you keep this full notice when you use the book.

You can find free copies of this book in multiple formats (web, PDF, EPUB) at: https://press.rebus.community/makingopentextbookswithstudents/.

Print ISBN: 978-1-989014-02-8

Ebook ISBN: 978-1-989014-03-5

Do you have comments about this book? Please visit http://bit.ly/OTwithstudents.

Rebus Community

This book was created with support from the Rebus Community for Open Textbook Creation, where we are building new collaborative models for creating & sustaining open textbooks. Would you like to collaborate on an open textbook? Join the Rebus Community at projects.rebus.community.

Are you a faculty member or administrator with questions about this book, or about open textbooks generally? Please get in touch with us at contact@rebus.community.

CONTENTS

Introduction	1
Contributors	iii

PART I. OPEN PEDAGOGY

1. Open Pedagogy — 7
   Robin DeRosa, director of interdisciplinary studies at Plymouth State University & Rajiv Jhangiani, University Teaching Fellow in Open Studies at Kwantlen Polytechnic University

PART II. PROJECT IDEAS & CASE STUDIES

2. Creating an Open Textbook — 23
3. Case Study: Frank Lloyd Wright and His Madison Buildings — 24
   Ed. Elizabeth Mays
4. Case study: Antología Abierta de Literatura Hispánica — 30
   Ed. Elizabeth Mays
5. Interview with David Squires: Social Media Texts — 34
   David Squires, visiting assistant professor at Washington State University
6. Student Spotlight: Samara Burns, Open Logic Project — 40
   Samara Burns, M.A. in philosophy student at University of Calgary

7. Interview with Gabriel Higginbotham, Open Oregon State — 43
Gabriel Higginbotham, IT consultant and recent-former student at Open Oregon State

8. Adapting an Open Textbook — 48

9. Case Study: Principles of Microeconomics — 49
Ed. Elizabeth Mays

10. Case Study: Expanding the Open Anthology of Earlier American Literature — 54
Timothy Robbins, assistant professor of English at Graceland University

11. Student Spotlight: Matthew Moore, The Open Anthology of Earlier American Literature, 2nd Edition — 66
Matthew Moore, English and studio art major at Graceland University

PART III. STUDENT RIGHTS & FACULTY RESPONSIBILITIES

12. Licensing — 71
13. Privacy & Anonymity — 75
14. Digital Literacy — 77
David Squires

PART IV. SAMPLE ASSIGNMENTS

15. Teaching Guide: Expand an Open Textbook — 83
Julie Ward, assistant professor of 20th and 21st-century Latin American literature at University of Oklahoma

16. Assignment: Create an Open Textbook — 93
Anna Andrzejewski, art history professor and director of graduate studies at the University of Wisconsin-Madison

Part V. Resources

17. CC Licensing Guide — 103
    Zoe Wake Hyde
18. MOU for Students and Faculty — 109
    Zoe Wake Hyde
19. Course: Becoming an Open Educator — 111
    Apurva Ashok

About the Publisher — 112
Licensing Information — 113
Other Open Textbooks Produced With Rebus Community Support — 115
As Seen In — 120

INTRODUCTION

At the Rebus Community, we are building a new, collaborative model of publishing for open textbooks.

Wrapped up in those words–new, collaborative, publishing, open–are some ambitious goals:

- We want to make it easier for a global community of open textbook practitioners from disparate institutions to find each other and collaborate on Open Educational Resources.
- We want to make the process of building or contributing to an open textbook easier.
- We want to make open textbooks in every subject in every language available free of charge and free of licensing restrictions in every format possible.

No doubt, growing the OER ecosystem on the creation side will make it easier for students to find and use open textbooks in their disciplines. But enabling students to contribute to open textbooks could transform them into even more accessible resources for learning.

Producing such resources hones research, writing, editing, teamwork, and digital literacy skills Moreover, such experiences can make class learning interactive—going from what one of our contributors describes as a "banking" model of class instruction into an "inquiry-based" and participatory model.[1]

---

1. Timothy Robbins, "Case Study: Expanding the Open Anthology of Earlier American

We're thrilled when we learn about faculty embarking on classroom projects that meet the class's objectives for student learning outcomes and engagement through projects that involve students in the research, compilation, and production of open textbooks.

This guide aims to both inspire and equip more faculty to follow in these Open Pedagogy pioneers' tracks in making open textbooks with students.

As with all Rebus open textbooks, this guide is but the first edition of a work designed to evolve, iterate, and expand. It is not complete–there are aspects we did not cover in this first edition–but we hope to fill these gaps going forward. If you have something to add, please let us know by commenting on the Guide to Making Open Textbooks With Students project[2] in the Rebus Community Forum.

Literature," *Guide to Making Open Textbooks With Students,* https://press.rebus.community/makingopentextbookswithstudents/chapter/case-study-expanding-open-anthology-of-earlier-american-literature/.

2. "Project: Making Open Textbooks With Students," *Rebus Community Forum,* https://forum.rebus.community/topic/119/project-summary-guide-to-making-open-textbooks-with-students/15.

CONTRIBUTORS

This handbook was compiled, edited and formatted by staff of the Rebus Community for Open Textbook Creation including **Elizabeth Mays**, **Zoe Wake Hyde** and **Apurva Ashok**.

It features essays by Open Pedagogy practitioners **Robin DeRosa**, director of interdisciplinary studies at Plymouth State University; **Rajiv Jhangiani**, University Teaching Fellow in Open Studies at Kwantlen Polytechnic University; **Timothy Robbins**, assistant professor of English at Graceland University; and **David Squires**, visiting assistant professor at Washington State University; sample assignments from **Anna Andrzejewski**, art history professor and director of graduate studies at the University of Wisconsin-Madison and **Julie Ward**, assistant professor of 20th and 21st-century Latin American literature at University of Oklahoma; and **Timothy Robbins**; as well as the voices of many other faculty and students engaged in open textbook projects. Among them:

- **Alice Barrett**, student at University of Oklahoma
- **Samara Burns**, student at University of Calgary
- **Amanda Coolidge**, senior manager of Open Education at BCcampus
- **Gabriel Higginbotham**, recent-former student at Open Oregon State
- **Matthew Moore**, student at Graceland University
- **Maxwell Nicholson**, student at University of Victoria

- **Steel Wagstaff**, instructional technology consultant at UW-Madison

We are grateful to all who contributed to this project.

If you would like to add to this guide for an expanded, second edition, please volunteer to add your voice to the project[1] in the Rebus Community Forum.

---

1. "Project: Making Open Textbooks With Students," *Rebus Community Forum*, https://forum.rebus.community/topic/119/project-summary-guide-to-making-open-textbooks-with-students/15.

PART I

OPEN PEDAGOGY

What is Open Pedagogy? How are professors practicing it in their classrooms to build open textbooks and other Open Educational Resources? What are the advantages to Open Pedagogy? This section answers these questions and provides ideas for working within existing teaching structures to introduce Open Pedagogy into your classes.

Chapter 1

OPEN PEDAGOGY

ROBIN DEROSA, DIRECTOR OF INTERDISCIPLINARY STUDIES AT PLYMOUTH STATE UNIVERSITY & RAJIV JHANGIANI, UNIVERSITY TEACHING FELLOW IN OPEN STUDIES AT KWANTLEN POLYTECHNIC UNIVERSITY

There are many ways to begin a discussion of "Open Pedagogy." Although providing a framing definition might be the obvious place to start, we want to resist that for just a moment to ask a set of related questions: What are your hopes for education, particularly for higher education? What vision do you work toward when you design your daily professional practices in and out of the classroom? How do you see the roles of the learner and the teacher? What challenges do your students face in their learning environments, and how does your pedagogy address them?

"Open Pedagogy," as we engage with it, is a site of praxis, a place where theories about learning, teaching, technology, and social justice enter into a conversation with each other and inform the development of educational practices and structures. This site is dynamic, contested, constantly under revision, and resists static definitional claims. But it is not a site vacant of meaning or political conviction. In this brief introduction, we offer a pathway for engaging with the current conversations around Open Pedagogy, some ideas about its philosophical foundation, investments, and its utility, and some concrete ways that students and teachers—all of us learners—can "open" education. We hope that this chapter will inspire those of us in education to focus our critical and aspirational lenses on larger questions about the ideology embedded within our educational systems and the ways in which pedagogy impacts these systems. At the same time we hope to provide some tools and techniques to those who want to build a more empowering, collaborative, and just architecture for learning.

"Open Pedagogy" as a named approach to teaching is nothing new. Scholars such as Catherine Cronin,[1] Katy Jordan,[2] Vivien Rolfe,[3] and Tannis Morgan have traced the term back to early etymologies. Morgan cites a 1979 article[4] by the Canadian Claude Paquette: "Paquette outlines three sets of foundational values of Open Pedagogy, namely: autonomy and interdependence; freedom and responsibility; democracy and participation."

Many of us who work with Open Pedagogy today have come into the conversations not only through an interest in the historical arc of the scholarship of teaching and learning, but also by way of Open Education, and specifically, by way of Open Educational Resources (OERs). OERs are educational materials that are openly-licensed, usually with Creative Commons licenses, and therefore they are generally characterized by the 5 Rs[5]: they can be reused, retained, redistributed, revised, and remixed. As conversations about teaching and learning developed around the

---

1. Catherine Cronin, "Opening Up Open Pedagogy," Catherine Cronin's professional website, April 24, 2017, http://catherinecronin.net/research/opening-up-open-pedagogy/.
2. Katy Jordan, "The History of Open Education", *shift+refresh* (blog), June 19, 2017, https://shiftandrefresh.wordpress.com/2017/06/19/the-history-of-open-education-a-timeline-and-bibliography/.
3. Vivien Rolfe, "OER18 Open to All," Vivien Rolfe's professional website, http://vivrolfe.com/books-and-publications/.
4. Tannis Morgan, "Open Pedagogy and a Very Brief History of the Concept," *Explorations in the EdTech World (blog)* Tannis Morgan's professional website, December 21, 2016, https://homonym.ca/uncategorized/open-pedagogy-and-a-very-brief-history-of-the-concept/.
5. David Wiley, "Defining the Open in Open Content and Open Educational Resources," *Opencontent.org*, http://opencontent.org/definition/.

experience of adopting and adapting OERs, the phrase "Open Pedagogy" began to re-emerge, this time crucially inflected with the same "open" that inflects the phrase "open license."

In this way, we can think about Open Pedagogy as a term that is connected to many teaching and learning theories that predate Open Education, but also as a term that is newly energized by its relationship to OERs and the broader ecosystem of open (Open Education, yes, but also Open Access, Open Science, Open Data, Open Source, Open Government, etc.). David Wiley, the Chief Academic Officer of Lumen Learning,[6] was one of the first OER-focused scholars who articulated how the use of OERs could transform pedagogy. He wrote in 2013 about the tragedy of "disposable assignments"[7] that "actually suck value out of the world," and he postulated not only that OERs offer a free alternative to high-priced commercial textbooks, but also that the open license would allow students (and teaching faculty) to contribute to the knowledge commons, not just consume from it, in meaningful and lasting ways. Recently, Wiley has revised his language to focus on "OER-Enabled Pedagogy,"[8] with an explicit commitment to foregrounding the 5R permissions and the ways that they transform teaching and learning.

As Wiley has focused on students-as-contributors and the role of OERs in education, other Open Pedagogues have widened the lens through which Open Pedagogy refracts. Mike Caulfield, for example, has argued[9] that while OER has been driving the car for a while, Open Pedagogy is in the backseat ready to hop over into the front. Caulfield sees the replacement of the proprietary textbook by OERs as a necessary step in enabling widespread institu-

---

6. *Lumenlearning.com*, http://lumenlearning.com/about/mission/.
7. David Wiley, "What is Open Pedagogy," *iterating toward openness*, October 21, 2013, https://opencontent.org/blog/archives/2975.
8. David Wiley, "OER-enabled Pedagogy," *iterating toward openness*, May 2, 2017, https://opencontent.org/blog/archives/5009.
9. Mike Caulfield, "Putting Student-Produced OER at the Heart of the Institution," *hapgood*, Mike Caulfield's professional website, Sept. 7, 2016, https://hapgood.us/2016/09/07/putting-student-produced-oer-at-the-heart-of-the-institution/.

tional open learning practice. In that post, Caulfield shorthands Open Pedagogy: "student blogs, wikis, etc." We might delve in a bit deeper here. Beyond participating in the creation of OERs via the 5 Rs, what exactly does it mean to engage in "Open Pedagogy?"

First, we want to recognize that Open Pedagogy shares common investments with many other historical and contemporary schools of pedagogy. For example, constructivist pedagogy, connected learning, and critical digital pedagogy are all recognizable pedagogical strands that overlap with Open Pedagogy. From constructivist pedagogy, particularly as it emerged from John Dewey and, in terms of its relationship to technology, from Seymour Papert, we recognize a critique of industrial and automated models for learning, a valuing of experiential and learner-centered inquiry, and a democratizing vision for the educational process. From connected learning, especially as it coheres in work supported by the *Digital Media and Learning Research Hub*,[10] we recognize a hope that human connections facilitated by technologies can help learners engage more fully with the knowledge and ideas that shape our world. And from critical digital pedagogy,[11] as developed by Digital Humanities-influenced thinkers at Digital Pedagogy Lab out of educational philosophy espoused by scholars such as Paulo Freire and bell hooks, we recognize a commitment to diversity, collaboration, and structural critique of both educational systems and the technologies that permeate them.

If we merge OER advocacy with the kinds of pedagogical approaches that focus on collaboration, connection, diversity, democracy, and critical assessments of educational tools and structures, we can begin to understand the breadth and power of Open Pedagogy as a guiding praxis. To do this, we need to

---

10. Digital Media and Learning Research Hub, https://dmlhub.net/.
11. Jesse Stommel, "Critical Digital Pedagogy: A Definition," *Digital Pedagogy Lab*, Nov. 18, 2014, http://www.digitalpedagogylab.com/hybridped/critical-digital-pedagogy-definition/.

link these pedagogical investments with the reality of the educational landscape as it now exists. The United Nations Universal Declaration of Human Rights[12] asserts that "higher education shall be equally accessible to all." Yet, even in North America in 2017, "the likelihood of earning a college degree is tied to family income" (Goldrick-Rab).[13] For those of us who work in higher ed, it's likely that we have been casually aware of the link between family income and college enrollment, attendance, persistence, and completion. But for those of us who teach, it's also likely that the pedagogies and processes that inflect our daily work are several steps removed from the economic challenges that our students face. Even though 67% of college students in Florida and 54% of those in British Columbia[14] cannot afford to purchase at least one of their required course textbooks, we more readily attribute their inability to complete assigned readings to laziness and entitlement than to unaffordability. This is precisely why the push to reduce the high cost of textbooks that has been the cornerstone of the OER movement has been a wake-up call for many of us who may not always have understood what we could do to directly impact the affordability of a college degree.

When faculty use OERs, we aren't just saving a student money on textbooks: we are directly impacting that student's ability to enroll in, persist through, and successfully complete a course.[15] In other words, we are directly impacting that student's ability to attend, succeed in, and graduate from college. When we talk about OERs, we bring two things into focus: that access

---

12. "Universal Declaration of Human Rights," *UN.org*, http://www.un.org/en/universal-declaration-human-rights/.
13. Sara Goldrick-Rab, Paying the Price: *College Costs, Financial Aid and the Betrayal of the American Dream* (Chicago: The University of Chicago Press, 2016).
14. Rajiv Sunil Jhangiani, Surita Jhangiani, "Investigating the Perceptions, Use, and Impact of Open Textbooks: A Survey of Post-Secondary Students in British Columbia," *The International Review of Research in Open and Distributed Learning* 18, no 4 (2017).
15. John Hilton III, Lane Fischer, David Wiley, and Linda Williams, "Maintaining Momentum Toward Graduation: OER and the Course Throughput Rate." *International Review of Research in Open and Distributed Learning* 17, no. 6 (December 2016), http://www.irrodl.org/index.php/irrodl/article/view/2686/3967.

is critically important to conversations about academic success, and that faculty and other instructional staff can play a critical role in the process of making learning accessible.

If a central gift that OERs bring to students is that they make college more affordable, one of the central gifts that they bring to faculty is that of agency, and how this can help us rethink our pedagogies in ways that center on access. If we do this, we might start asking broader questions that go beyond "How can I lower the cost of textbooks in this course?" If we think of ourselves as responsible for making sure that everyone can come to our course table to learn, we will find ourselves concerned with the many other expenses that students face in paying for college. How will they get to class if they can't afford gas money or a bus pass? How will they afford childcare on top of tuition fees? How will they focus on their homework if they haven't had a square meal in two days or if they don't know where they will be sleeping that night? How will their families pay rent if they cut back their work hours in order to attend classes? How much more student loan debt will they take on for each additional semester it takes to complete all of their required classes? How will they obtain the credit card they need to purchase an access code? How will they regularly access their free open textbook if they don't own an expensive laptop or tablet?

And what other access issues do students face as they face these economic challenges? Will they be able to read their Chemistry textbook given their vision impairment? Will their LMS site list them by their birth name rather than their chosen name, and thereby misgender them? Will they have access to the knowledge they need for research if their college restricts their search access or if they don't have Wi-Fi or a computer at home? Are they safe to participate in online, public collaborations if they are undocumented? Is their college or the required adaptive learning platform collecting data on them, and if so, could those data be used in ways that could put them at risk?

OERs invite faculty to play a direct role in making higher education more accessible. And they invite faculty to ask questions about how we can impact access in ways that go beyond textbook costs. At the very least, they help us see the challenges that students face in accessing higher education as broad, as severe, and as directly related to their academic success, or lack thereof.

So one key component of Open Pedagogy might be that it sees access, broadly writ, as fundamental to learning and to teaching, and agency as an important way of broadening that access. OERs are licensed with open licenses, which reflects not just a commitment to access in terms of the cost of knowledge, but also access in terms of the creation of knowledge. Embedded in the social justice commitment to making college affordable for all students is a related belief that knowledge should not be an elite domain. Knowledge consumption and knowledge creation are not separate but parallel processes, as knowledge is co-constructed, contextualized, cumulative, iterative, and recursive. In this way, Open Pedagogy invites us to focus on how we can increase access to higher education and how we can increase access to knowledge–both its reception and its creation. This is, fundamentally, about the dream of a public learning commons, where learners are empowered to shape the world as they encounter it. With the open license at the heart of our work, we care both about "free" and about "freedom," about resources and practices, about access and about accessibility, about content and about contribution. This is not a magical thinking[16] approach to digital pedagogy. It's an honest appraisal of the barriers that exist in our educational systems and a refusal to abdicate responsibility for those barriers.

To summarize, we might think about Open Pedagogy as an access-oriented commitment to learner-driven education AND as a process of designing architectures and using tools for learning that enable students to shape the public knowledge commons

---

16. Nicole Mirra, "What Do We Mean When We Talk About 21st Century Learning?" *dmlcentral*, https://dmlcentral.net/mean-talk-21st-century-learning/#.WSb0VJg29TQ.twitter.

of which they are a part. We might insist on the centrality of the 5 Rs to this work, and we might foreground the investments that Open Pedagogy shares with other learner-centered approaches to education. We might reconstitute Open Pedagogy continually, as our contexts shift and change and demand new, site-specific articulations. But if we want to begin "open" our courses, programs, and/or institutions, what practical steps can we take to get started?

OEP, or Open Educational Practices, can be defined as the set of practices that accompany either the use of OERs or, more to our point, the adoption of Open Pedagogy. Here are some simple but profoundly transformative examples of OEPs:

- Adapt or remix OERs with your students. Even the simple act of adding problem sets or discussion questions to an existing open textbook will help contribute to knowledge, to the quality of available OERs, and to your students' sense of doing work that matters. The adaptation of the open textbook Project Management for Instructional Designers[17] by successive cohorts of graduate students at Brigham Young University provides an excellent example of this approach.

- Build OERs with your students. Though students may be beginners with most of the content in your course, they are often more adept than you at understanding what beginning students need in order to understand the material. Asking students to help reframe and re-present course content in new and inventive ways can add valuable OERs to the commons while also allowing for the work that students do in courses to go on to have meaningful impact once the course ends. Consider the examples of the open textbook Environmental Science Bites[18] written by undergraduate students at the

---

17. Wiley, et al., *Project Management for Instructional Designers* (2016). https://pm4id.org/.

Ohio State University or the brief explainer videos[19] created by Psychology students around the world and curated by the NOBA Project.

- Teach your students how to edit Wikipedia articles. By adding new content, revising existing content, adding citations, or adding images, students can (with the support of the Wiki Education Foundation[20]) make direct contributions to one of the most popular public repositories for information. Indeed, more than 22,000 students already have, including medical students at the University of California San Francisco.[21] More than developing digital literacy and learning how to synthesize, articulate, and share information, students engage with and understand the politics of editing, including how "truth" is negotiated by those who have access to the tools that shape it.

- Facilitate student-created and student-controlled learning environments. The Learning Management System (Canvas, Moodle, Blackboard, etc.) generally locks students into closed environments that prevent sharing and collaboration outside of the class unit; it perpetuates a surveillance model of education in which the instructor is able to consider metrics that students are not given access to; and it presupposes that all student work is disposable (as all of it will be deleted when the new course shell is imported for the next semester). Initiatives such as Domain of One's Own[22] enable students to build "personal

---

18. Kylienne A. Clark, Travis R. Shaul, and Brian H. Lower, eds., *Environmental ScienceBites* (Columbus: The Ohio State University, 2015).
19. "2016-17 Noba + Psi Chi Student Video Award Recipients," *NOBA*, http://nobaproject.com/student-video-award/winners.
20. "Teach With Wikipedia," *Wiki Education Foundation*, https://wikiedu.org/teach-with-wikipedia/.
21. Eryk Salvaggio, "For Wikipedia, the Doctor Is in ... Class," *WikiEdu*, April 5, 2016, https://wikiedu.org/blog/2016/04/05/medical-students-wikipedia/.
22. *Domain of One's Own*, http://umw.domains/.

cyberinfrastructures"[23] where they can manage their own learning, control their own data, and design home ports that can serve as sites for collaboration and conversation about their work. Students can choose to openly license the work that they post on these sites, thereby contributing OERs to the commons; they can also choose not to openly license their work, which is an exercising of their rights and perfectly in keeping with the ethos of Open Pedagogy. If students create their own learning architectures, they can (and should) control how public or private they wish to be, how and when to share or license their work, and what kinds of design, tools, and plug-ins will enhance their learning. It is important to point out here that open is not the opposite of private.

- Encourage students to apply their expertise to serve their community. Partner with nonprofit organizations to create opportunities for students to apply their research or marketing skills.[24] Or ask them to write (and submit for publication) op-ed pieces[25] to share evidence-based approaches to tackling a local social problem. Demonstrate the value of both knowledge application and service by scaffolding their entry into public scholarship.

- Engage students in public chats with authors or experts. Platforms such as Twitter can help engage students in scholarly and professional conversations with practitioners in their fields. This is another way that students can contribute to—not just consume—knowledge, and it shifts learning into a

23. Gardner Campbell, "A Personal Cyberinfrastructure," *EduCause Review* 44, no. 5 (September 4, 2009), http://er.educause.edu/articles/2009/9/a-personal-cyberinfrastructure.
24. Lori Rosenthal, "Research for Community Action," *Action Teaching*, http://www.actionteaching.org/award/community-action.
25. "Assignment Type: Op-Ed," *Kent State Online,* http://onlineteaching.kent.edu/library/online_assignments/OpEd_Handout.pdf.

dialogic experience. In addition, if students are sharing work publicly, they can also use social media channels to drive mentors, teachers, peers, critics, experts, friends, family, and the public to their work for comment. Opening conversations about academic and transdisciplinary work—both student work and the work of established scholars and practitioners—is, like contributing to OERs, a way to grow a thriving knowledge commons.

- Build course policies, outcomes, assignments, rubrics, and schedules of work collaboratively with students. Once we involve students in creating or revising OERs or in shaping learning architectures, we can begin to see the syllabus as more of a collaborative document, co-generated at least in part with our students. Can students help craft course policies that would support their learning, that they feel more ownership over? Can they add or revise course learning outcomes in order to ensure the relevancy of the course to their future paths? Can they develop assignments for themselves and/or their classmates, and craft rubrics to accompany them to guide an evaluative process? Can they shape the course schedule according to rhythms that will help maximize their efforts and success?

- Let students curate course content. Your course is likely split into a predictable number of units (fourteen, for example) to conform to the academic calendar of the institution within which the course is offered. We would probably all agree that such segmenting of our fields is somewhat arbitrary; there is nothing ontological about Introduction to Psychology being fourteen weeks long (or spanning twenty-eight textbook chapters, etc.). And when we select a novel for a course on postcolonial literature or a lab exercise for Anatomy and Physiology, we are aware that there are a multitude of other good options for each that we could have chosen. We can involve students in the process of curating content for courses, either by offering them limited choices between different texts or by offering them solid time to curate a future unit more or less on their own (or in a group) as a research project. The content of a course may be somewhat prescribed by accreditation or field standards, but within those confines, we can involve students in the curation process, increasing the level of investment they have with the content while helping them acquire a key twenty-first century skill.

- Ask critical questions about "open." When you develop new pathways based on Open Pedagogy, pay special attention to the barriers, challenges, and problems that emerge. Be explicit about them, honest about them, and share them widely with others working in Open Education so that we can work together to make improvements. Being an open educator in this fashion is especially crucial if we wish to avoid digital redlining,[26] creating inequities (however unintentionally) through the use of technology. Ask yourself: Do your students have access to broadband at home? Do they have the laptops or tablets they need to easily access and engage with OERs? Do they have the supports they need to experiment creatively, often for the first time, with technology tools? Do they have the digital literacies they need to ensure as much as is possible their safety and privacy online? Do you have a full understanding of the terms of service of the EdTech tools you are using in your courses? As you work to increase the accessibility of your own course, are you also evaluating the tools

---

26. Chris Gilliard, "Pedagogy and the Logic of Platforms," *Educause Review*, July 3, 2017, http://er.educause.edu/articles/2017/7/pedagogy-and-the-logic-of-platforms.

and technologies[27] you are using to ask how they help or hinder your larger vision for higher education?

These are just a few ideas for getting started with Open Pedagogy. Most important, find people to talk with about your ideas. Ask questions about how OERs and the 5 Rs change the nature of a course or the relationships that students have to their learning materials. Look to programs and colleges that are widely accessible and which serve a broad variety of learners and ask questions about how their course designs are distinct or compelling. Ask your students about meaningful academic contributions they have made, and what structures were in place that facilitated those contributions. Try, explore, fail, share, revise.

Open Pedagogy is not a magical panacea for the crises that currently challenge higher ed. That being said, we both feel that Open Pedagogy offers a set of dynamic commitments that could help faculty and students articulate a sustainable, vibrant, and inclusive future for our educational institutions. By focusing on access, agency, and a commons-oriented approach to education, we can clarify our challenges and firmly assert a learner-centered vision for higher education.

A portion of this article was remixed from "Open Pedagogy and Social Justice" by Rajiv Jhangiani and Robin DeRosa, available under a CC-BY 4.0 license at http://www.digitalpedagogy-lab.com/open-pedagogy-social-justice/.[28]

Robin DeRosa *is director of interdisciplinary studies at Plymouth State University, part of the university system of New Hampshire. Her current research and advocacy work focuses on Open Education, and how universities can innovate in order to bring down costs for students, increase interdisciplinary collaboration, and refocus the academic world*

---

27. Jesse Stommel, "Critically Evaluating Digital Tools," *Digital Studies 101*, https://dgst101.com/activity-critically-evaluating-digital-tools-3f60d468ce74.
28. Rajiv Jhangiani and Robin DeRosa, "Open Pedagogy and Social Justice," *Digital Pedagogy Lab*, June 2, 2017, http://www.digitalpedagogylab.com/open-pedagogy-social-justice/.

on strengthening the public good. She is also an editor for Hybrid Pedagogy, an open-access, peer-reviewed journal that combines the strands of critical pedagogy and digital pedagogy to arrive at the best social and civil uses for technology and new media in education.

Rajiv Jhangiani is the University Teaching Fellow in Open Studies and a faculty member in the Department of Psychology at Kwantlen Polytechnic University. He also serves as an Open Education Advisor with BCcampus and an associate editor of Psychology Learning and Teaching. Previously he served as an OER Research Fellow with the Open Education Group, a faculty fellow with the BC Open Textbook Project, a faculty workshop facilitator with the Open Textbook Network, and the associate editor of NOBA Psychology.

PART II

PROJECT IDEAS & CASE STUDIES

Are you considering embarking on an Open Pedagogy project in your classroom? These projects will inspire you!

Chapter 2

CREATING AN OPEN TEXTBOOK

We talked to faculty and students who have worked on open textbook projects in their classrooms recently. The next section consists of case studies, interviews, and firsthand essays highlighting seminal examples of Open Pedagogy projects.

Chapter 3

CASE STUDY: FRANK LLOYD WRIGHT AND HIS MADISON BUILDINGS

ED. ELIZABETH MAYS

Anna Andrzejewski, an art history professor and director of graduate studies at the University of Wisconsin-Madison, was looking for a hands-on learning project for her Frank Lloyd Wright art history course.

The class was an upper-division, research course designed for art history majors or grad students, but also open to other disciplines. Andrzejewski had arranged access to seven historic local Frank Lloyd Wright houses for the course.

Known for hands-on learning projects that used student research to get ideas out into the broader community, she had had her students create walking tour booklets and websites documenting architectural landmarks in previous courses, but for this class she wanted to do something different.

Steel Wagstaff, an instructional technology consultant at the university, approached her with the idea of having the students create a book using Pressbooks,[1] an online book-formatting software often used for open textbook projects.

Because Frank Lloyd Wright was not her primary area of schol-

---

1. *Pressbooks.com*, https://pressbooks.com/.

arship, Andrzejewski said, the project became an opportunity for her to learn along with the students.

"Part of the appeal of working on this textbook idea was to create something that the students would participate in and feel invested in but that I could also use later on as a tool in future classes."

Wagstaff said the project was designed to be a "renewable assignment," one whose life extended beyond the term of the class.

"What I saw the students really engage with was the idea that they're writing this for Anna but also for a public audience," Wagstaff said.

Knowing that the next time Andrzejewski taught the course, her students would read the previous students' writing and could add to it or could improve it deepened student engagement with the project, Wagstaff said.

In addition, students might not have access to the same private homes featured in the book in future semesters.

"We hope that this book will provide surrogate access to many of these places for future classes, since they likely won't be able to visit all of them when the course is taught in future semesters," Wagstaff said.

Before embarking on the major assignment, Andrzejewski gave the students a lower-stakes, small-scale assignment that helped them learn how to use Pressbooks. Each student had to write several paragraphs of architectural context for the building they would visit and upload images into the platform for an overview section framing the progression of Frank Lloyd Wright's career.

From the low-stakes assignment, Andrzejewski said, "They saw what they had to do. It involved them and also scared them such that they were invested for the rest of the time."

Next, the small class of cross-disciplinary students, which included journalism, art, history, geography, urban planning, and other majors, made field visits to seven local Frank Lloyd Wright homes that Andrzejewski had arranged access to.

Making a real book, noted Wagstaff, involves knowledge from lots of different disciplines, and the students in Andrzejewski's class were able to have cross-functional conversations as they built it.

"It was different than 'everyone's writing their own research paper and they never talk to each other,'" Wagstaff said.

At each home they visited, students all had the same shared experience, but two or three took ownership to document that home for a chapter of the book. Those students asked the others for feedback during and after the site visit on what they found most interesting and what they should write about. Students got to pick a theme for each chapter.

"There's nothing wrong with having an assignment that's based on what you do in class, but it's how to make it more than just a report and how to take it in a new direction," Andrzejewski said.

From an instructional design perspective, Wagstaff said that before students do a site visit, they need to have a sense for what the product is going to be so they can develop research questions in preparation.

Andrzejewski gave her students flexibility within constraints for the group textbook assignment.

First and foremost, the assignment specified that each chapter must include a theme appropriate to the home featured. For instance: preservation, a period of Wright's career, modular design, or a style of architecture.

In addition, the assignment specified that each chapter should include three different sections:

- An introduction, a one- to two-paragraph overview of the house, and a thesis statement of the chapter to follow;
- An architectural description of the building, to include three to five paragraphs of description and complementary images; and
- An interpretive thematic section, which was a minimum-three-paragraph, "abundantly illustrated" narrative that was to demonstrate evidence that they listened to their classmates at the class discussions at the site and that they had done additional research outside of class. (Sources for this research could include anything from oral histories to archival research, book research or interviews.)

Students did all the writing, image collection and uploading, editing, book styling and footnotes as they built the book.

The chapters ended up being very different, rather than uniform as in a typical textbook, which could be considered a strength or a weakness.

"[The chapters] follow a basic research model. They all have footnotes and they all have pictures. But the approaches they take to these buildings are pretty disparate," Wagstaff said.

As of this writing, Andrzejewski and Wagstaff still have work to do over the summer to clean up the book, which is not yet public, in order to make it ready for public view. It will need editing and they'll have to remove images that were not openly licensed, which are fair use for educational purposes, but not fair game for publication.

The next time, Andrzejewski said, she'll make using open images a requirement, and build in a week of collaborative editing in the last week of class.

Wagstaff said they will also build in more interactivity in the editing and on the images themselves.

In terms of the content, Wagstaff said he noticed two differences between this and similar Open Pedagogy projects.

First, students used lots of footnotes, and many of them cited not just websites or books but personal interviews with experts and working professionals.

"These weren't just surface-level quotes. These were substantive conversations they had with real people," Wagstaff said, remarking on "the depth of engagement they had with actual knowledgeable working professionals."

Andrzejewski attributes this to the interview training she incorporated with an oral historian before students embarked on the project.

Second, they did a lot of high-quality documentation in the form of photographs rather than just using photos they could find online.

Andrzejewski said the students got inspired by the possibilities for including media after doing the preliminary assignment in Pressbooks.

"They really wanted to be creators of evidence not just regurgitating it," Andrzejewski said.

She said she felt the project was successful and is now thinking about a similar project for a different class.

"I was so pleased with it I want to do something like it again," Andrzejewski said.

Wagstaff added: "What all instructors want is higher buyin–higher engagement from their learners. A project like this almost by its very nature produces that."

KEY TAKEAWAYS

- Partner with community organizations, so that your project has an impact beyond the classroom.

- Give students small assignments that help them build confidence and acquire the skills needed to complete a larger, final assignment.

- Clearly communicate license requirements for images, videos, or other materials that might be included in the textbook.

- Encourage your students to look beyond literature (on the Internet or on paper) when conducting research. Suggest they conduct interviews with working professionals or other experts in the field.

- Build in time within the semester to collaboratively edit and refine the final product.

Chapter 4

CASE STUDY: ANTOLOGÍA ABIERTA DE LITERATURA HISPÁNICA

ED. ELIZABETH MAYS

Antología Abierta de Literatura Hispánica (*The Introduction to Hispanic Literature*) is the brainchild of Dr. Julie Ward, an assistant professor of twentieth- and twenty-first-century Latin American literature at University of Oklahoma.

Ward said the anthology was inspired by *The Open Anthology of Earlier American Literature*[1] project Robin DeRosa spearheaded in her classroom. When she saw that text, she thought, "That's exactly what I wanted to do."

In the fall 2016 semester, she embarked on a project in her Spanish-language literature course, Introduction to Hispanic Literature and Culture, in which groups of four to five students selected ten texts from the fifteenth century to the twentieth century to include in a critical edition.

The included texts span different genres of literature, with authors ranging from Christopher Columbus to Horacio Quiroga. Ward and a graduate student "research guide" had pre-established lists of texts students could review and choose from.

For each work, the student groups compiled context in the form

---

1. Robin DeRosa, *The Open Anthology of Earlier American Literature* (Public Commons Publishing: 2015). https://openamlit.pressbooks.com/.

of an introduction, at least ten annotations on the text about style, references and colloquialisms, an image and a biography about the author–their style, milieux and how the work relates to the rest of their works, and a bibliography. The texts, introductions and all other contextual elements of the book are all in Spanish.

The content of the critical edition was developed in the class, but the work on the text didn't end there. In the subsequent semester, two students were paid to take the critical edition, verify the facts and public domain licenses, and format it using Pressbooks. Alice Barrett, who is being paid by the OU Office of Undergraduate Research, is one of these students. The other student, Karlee Bradberry, is an honors research assistant, funded through the OU Honors College Research Assistant Program.

"I had a great experience with the group work aspect of the project," said Barrett, who said Ward emphasized group dynamics and started class with an article about a study Google had done about creating groups of people that work efficiently and creatively.

"For me what was most helpful was Dr. Ward's organizational skills. It was very clear what we were expected to do."

Barrett said she learned a lot from the project, including how to do research to find information, how to leverage library resources, and how to split the workload in a group. (She noted you have to let people do the work that's assigned to them.)

Projects like this "will be successful if the group dynamic is successful and everyone knows what they're going to be working on," she said.

She recommends that future instructors considering similar projects make sure their students find sources in the public domain and cite their sources thoroughly and correctly.

After working on the project Barrett said she feels more confident about taking on big projects as well as writing in Spanish. In her work after the class, she edited and verified sources for "Hombres necios que acusáis" by Sor Juana Inés de la Cruz, one of the first feminist writers in Spanish literature. That experience really influenced her perspective.

"I have a perspective on Spanish literature I didn't have before. It changes you."

When released, the book will be appropriate for university Spanish and Latin American literature courses as well as AP Spanish students in high school.

Currently the book is receiving support from the Rebus Community to create a replicable assignment that will allow Ward's peers at other universities to do similar projects in their classes to expand the text (view the assignment); to find Spanish speakers to edit and proofread the book; and to enlist faculty to beta-test the book in their courses and provide feedback to Ward on improvements and revisions.

To join the project, go to http://bit.ly/openAALH.[2]

> ### KEY TAKEAWAYS
>
> - Look to your peers for inspiration! You may find their projects can be replicated in your classroom.
> - Inform your students if they must find public domain sources, and if possible, direct them toward some repositories. Teach them how to properly cite these sources up front.
> - Survey funding options such as research grants and work-study programs in order to obtain ongoing

---

2. "Project Summary: Guide to Making Open Textbooks With Students," *Rebus Community Forum,* http://bit.ly/openAALH

student help with the project after the semester is complete.

- Set clear expectations with your students: What are the final deliverables they need to submit?

- Be organized. Take your students through the project timeline when you first start out, and try to stick to it!

- Conduct regular check-ins with students to assess the group dynamics. Use this time to track the project's progress and ensure that everyone is aware of what is going on and where the project is headed.

CHAPTER 5

INTERVIEW WITH DAVID SQUIRES: SOCIAL MEDIA TEXTS

DAVID SQUIRES, VISITING ASSISTANT PROFESSOR AT WASHINGTON STATE UNIVERSITY

David Squires was a visiting assistant professor teaching in Washington State University's Digital Technology & Culture[1] program and works at the Center for Digital Scholarship and Curation.[2] In fall 2016, he had students in his Intro to Digital Technology & Culture course create two OER texts on social media, *The Social Construction of Media: Social Media, Culture and Everyday Life*[3] and *Everything You Ever Wanted to Know About Social Media (but Were Too Afraid to Ask)*.[4] We interviewed David about his experience.

TELL US ABOUT THE PROJECT:

The end product is meant to be a prototype of a OER textbook on social media. There are lots of marketing textbooks on social media, but nothing quite like a cultural studies textbook, so that was the goal: a model for what a social media textbook could look like.

1. "Digital Technology and Culture," *Washington State University,* https://dtc.wsu.edu/.
2. Center for Digital Scholarship and Curation, *Washington State University,* http://cdsc.libraries.wsu.edu/.
3. "The Social Construction of Media: Social Media, Culture and Everyday Life," http://scalar.usc.edu/works/cultures-of-social-media/index.
4. "Everything You Ever Wanted to Know About Social Media (but Were Too Afraid to Ask)," http://scalar.usc.edu/works/everything-you-always-wanted-to-know-about-social-media-but-were-too-afraid-to-ask/index.

HOW DID THE PROJECT UNFOLD?

We dedicated about six weeks to the whole thing. First we read, wrote, and discussed copyright, Creative Commons, and open access publishing. Then the students started researching topics and writing. Finally, they put the pieces together as a Scalar[5] book.

WHAT ROLE DID STUDENTS PLAY IN THE PROJECT?

My students did most everything, start to finish. I played the role of project manager but tried to let them do as much of the work as possible. They rose to the occasion, tackling research, writing, layout and design—they even conceptualized the subject areas and structure of the project. At the end, they presented their work in public, for the beginning of Open Access Week. That gave them a sense of a hard deadline that wasn't just me saying *due date*! It really was a moment in time that required a certain level of achievement. I'm glad to report that each chapter-group met the challenge, although a few individual students were not able to present.

HOW DID YOU LEVERAGE THE PROJECT TO ACHIEVE THE LEARNING OBJECTIVES FOR THE CLASS?

Over the past year, The DTC program at WSU has worked to clarify course objectives for "Intro to Digital Technology & Culture." Here's the outcome:

1. Perform humanistic inquiry in combination with computational methods.
2. Assess information and sources.
3. Engage in collaborative and project-based learning.
4. Practice creative design and analysis of digital media.

---

5. Scalar, *The Alliance for Networking Visual Culture*, http://scalar.usc.edu/scalar/.

THIS PROJECT FURTHERS EACH OF THESE OBJECTIVES:

1. Students learn digital research tools and a new web publishing platform, Scalar.
2. Students learn to assess sources as they research their specific chapters, especially as they pull web materials to feature in their book. A big part of this project was identifying valid primary and secondary sources, and knowing which were which.
3. They created this project as a class, and each chapter had a group of three students contributing.
4. The primary sources required critical analysis, while the Scalar platform allowed students to practice design and layout as part of the writing process.

WHAT ADVICE WOULD YOU HAVE FOR FACULTY PLANNING SIMILAR PROJECTS IN WHICH THEY AND STUDENTS CREATE OPEN TEXTBOOKS?

While I was writing the syllabus, six weeks seemed like a long time to work on a single project. During the semester, however, I wished we'd had more time. If I did it again, I think I would organize the copyright and open access material into one project. Then let the social media textbook follow as the second project. Which is a way of saying, I'd dedicate more time to the research and writing on social media. Research and writing can't be rushed, especially when students are learning a new platform.

The other note I would add is that Scalar worked very well for this assignment in all regards except one—multiple users working on the same page at the same time caused havoc. We made it work, but knowing that in advance would have helped me prepare students. In general, knowing the platform in advance is essential to guiding students through the process.

IF YOU DID THIS AGAIN, WHAT WOULD YOU CHANGE? WHAT ARE SOME PITFALLS FACULTY CAN WATCH OUT FOR?

In addition to the above advice, I'd suggest reading Anne Cong-Huyen's blog post, "Whittier Workshop: Scalar in the Classroom."[6] I wish I'd found it before teaching this assignment. She lays out the pros and cons of using Scalar very clearly, reminding readers early on that Scalar is a publishing platform, not a learning management system. I think it's important to emphasize the publishing, editing, and document design aspects of using Scalar. That should be part of the assignment goals when asking students to produce open textbooks.

I'M NOT SEEING INDIVIDUAL CREDITS FOR THE STUDENTS ON EACH CHAPTER, BUT I DO SEE THEM AT THE END CREDITED WITH THE WORK OVERALL. HOW DID THIS DECISION COME ABOUT?

The students who worked on those Scalar projects had varying degrees of interest in having their names attached. Some wanted to a byline on their writing; others wanted to remain anonymous. In the end, the class decided to create a contributors page for two reasons. First, because it prevented inconsistencies that would arise with some portions having bylines while others not. Second, after workshops, revisions, and collaborative writing they realized that a byline might not make a lot of sense. In the end, most students decided not to add their names to the contributors page and, if I recall, at least one decided to add her byline to a page she felt her own.

DID YOU HAVE ANY CONVERSATIONS ABOUT WHICH LICENSE TO USE WITH THE STUDENTS, AND WHAT WAS THE OUTCOME?

We did talk about licensing. We spent the first two weeks of the project discussing Creative Commons and selections of Lawrence Lessig's *Free Culture*. We were lucky enough to have WSU's scholarly communications librarian Talea Anderson[7] join us for one class period. She showed the students about twenty different open textbooks that she had on hand and asked them to look at the different licenses they used. Most used some version

---

6. Anne Cong-Huyen, "Whittier Workshop, Scalar in the Classroom," Anne Cong-Huyen's professional website, https://anitaconchita.wordpress.com/whittierworkshop/.
7. "Open Educational Resources," *WSU Projects*, http://cdsc.libraries.wsu.edu/research/wsu-projects/.

of a CC license but a couple had GNU licenses. That exercise was especially helpful for thinking about why some restrictions—like the non-commercial option—do not work for OER despite aligning with the spirit of creating affordable textbook options. In the end, the students decided they did not need a CC license. I was a little disappointed. However, they reasoned that using Scalar made it unnecessary because public Scalar books are easy to reproduce within Scalar but difficult to reproduce in any other form. They saw their prototypes as open (in the OER sense) to a only small community of Scalar users.

DID YOU DISCOVER ANYTHING UNEXPECTED IN THIS PROCESS?

I learned a lot about social media in the process of this assignment. My students had a lot of knowledge to share that didn't fully emerge during class discussion. Reading their chapters taught me that class discussion is the tip of the iceberg when it comes to what students have to share about a topic related to an important part of their everyday experience. Seeing students struggle with Scalar also taught me that frustration isn't necessarily bad. The students who experienced the most frustration were the same students who used the platform to its fullest capacities. Their chapters featured more interesting layouts, richer media, and better organization than the students who treated Scalar like just another blogging platform. The trick is to convince students to embrace the frustration!

KEY TAKEAWAYS

- Devote ample time for the research and writing stages.
- Familiarize yourself with the various platforms you will be using before the project begins. This will be necessary to assist and guide students through the project.

- Have students decide how to credit and license their contributions.

- To help students make informed decisions, invite a librarian in for a "guest lecture" on content licensing and attribution, and ask them to introduce students to the resources available at your institution. If these staff cannot come to the classroom, connect students to approach them as needed.

- If possible, have your students present their work to a public audience and/or look for a related event or celebration. This has a two-fold benefit: it gives students a deadline-in-disguise, and imbues them with a feeling of accomplishment.

- When coming up with new assignments or projects, map them to the learning objectives already laid out for your course.

- Encourage students to express their frustration when they experience roadblocks or obstacles. Offer what support you can, and help them see problems in a different perspective.

CHAPTER 6

STUDENT SPOTLIGHT: SAMARA BURNS, OPEN LOGIC PROJECT

SAMARA BURNS, M.A. IN PHILOSOPHY STUDENT AT UNIVERSITY OF CALGARY

Throughout my graduate degree I had the opportunity to work as a student assistant for the Open Logic Project. The project began in the philosophy department of my home institution, The University of Calgary, and was motivated by the lack of intermediate logic textbooks available for professors to use. Those textbooks that were available were very expensive, and often confusing for students who were relatively new to logic. In response to this issue, the Open Logic Project created a collaborative, customizable open-source textbook.[1] This kind of book has several advantages over traditional textbooks. Formal logic makes use of mathematical symbolism, but the symbols used vary from book to book. The customizable features of the Open Logic textbook allow faculty to choose the symbols that they wish to use. The book also gives instructors the ability to change the content as they see fit, and students do not have to pay for an electronic copy.

The book is written in LaTeX and stored on Github. Typesetting in LaTeX makes the customization aspect of the textbook easier. Important symbols and words have been tagged throughout the

---

1. Andy Arana, Jeremy Avigad, Walter Dean, Gillian Russell, Nicole Wyatt, Audrey Yap, and Richard Zach, eds. *Open Logic Project* (University of Calgary Faculty of Arts and the Campus Alberta OER Initiative: (2017), http://openlogicproject.org/.

text and, if a faculty adopting the textbook wishes to change a certain symbol or word, they can simply alter one line of code rather than searching the entire document. Adding or removing chapters from the book is just as easy. The Github platform gives others the ability to make changes and "push" them to the main hub if they feel those changes benefit the textbook overall. The collaborative nature of the project means that the book is continually being updated, expanded, and improved upon.

The project was instigated by my master's thesis supervisor, and I was one of several student assistants hired to help develop the text. I worked on several chapters in the textbook. In most instances, I was given class notes from professors affiliated with the project and was responsible for converting them into cohesive chapters. Each chapter turned out to be about fifteen pages in length. I was not only required to translate the notes into appropriate sentence/paragraph structure, but because of the format of the book, I had to remember to tag key words and symbols in order to accommodate customization. This led to some technical difficulties along the way. As the chapters progressed, new challenges would arise, such as the need to create and integrate diagrams into the chapters. This required extra research and time to execute correctly.

Ultimately, the key to success on the project, for me, was open communication with the two professors I was working with, and clear communication regarding expectations and deadlines. In addition to this, getting feedback on my work was extremely important, and I had to give myself enough time to make extensive revisions to my pieces. I discovered that writing a textbook is a different experience than writing an academic essay. The editing process was extensive, and was done both in-person and through email. In-person meetings were helpful, as we sat down down with a physical copy of the chapter and determined what sections needed revision or expansion. The GitHub platform facilitated online editing, as my professors had access to my work as I uploaded it. They could edit the chapters directly or contact me with their feedback.

My experience with the Open Logic Project has given me a new appreciation for teaching. I was lucky enough to have the opportunity to TA for a course where the book was used. This gave me the opportunity to see how students were responding to the text and gather feedback from them. Student feedback was used to improve the textbook at the end of the semester and the changes were published on GitHub. Being part of the project gave me tremendous insight into which elements of a textbook are most important for student learning, which will be valuable knowledge as I continue to teach in the future.

> **KEY TAKEAWAYS**
>
> - When conceiving a new project idea, look for existing gaps in the textbooks available for your field.
> - Get graduate students involved!
> - Clearly communicate your expectations and deadlines.
> - Give students feedback about their work at various stages of the project.
> - If you are using an open textbook in your classroom, don't discount the feedback your receive on it from students. Try to contact the textbook creators if you discover elements that need editing or updating.

Samara Burns *is currently finishing her master's degree in philosophy at the University of Calgary, where she studies formal logic. She plans to pursue a Ph.D. in 2018.*

Chapter 7

INTERVIEW WITH GABRIEL HIGGINBOTHAM, OPEN OREGON STATE

GABRIEL HIGGINBOTHAM, IT CONSULTANT AND RECENT-FORMER STUDENT AT OPEN OREGON STATE

Gabe Higginbotham worked as a student project assistant on open textbooks for two years at Open Oregon State. He received his B.S. in Business Information Systems at Oregon State in early 2017. Currently, he works as an IT consultant for OOS. In fall 2018, he will go to grad school abroad to study Human Computer Interaction Design. In his career, he plans to continue contributing to the Open Education field.

TELL US ABOUT THE ROLE YOU PLAYED IN OPEN TEXTBOOK CREATION AT OPEN OREGON STATE.

I have been involved with the creation of roughly 10 textbooks at Open Oregon State, including *A Primer for Computational Biology* (set to go to print soon!), *Introduction to Permaculture* and *Introduction to Microbiology*.

I worked on converting professors' texts (either Word or LaTeX) to HTML.

Some of our books were created from materials used in online courses; others were LaTeX books that became online books to increase their availability.

I also designed the books (using CSS) to cater to either the needs of the professor or the purposes of the book. I learned HTML, CSS, and LaTeX on the job, and was one of the first student workers in the department.

Books at Open Oregon State are created using PressBooks, a WordPress plugin. We use some other multimedia tools including video and, more recently, H5P. We also use a number of WordPress plugins such as a glossary, code highlighter, and broken link checker.

When I was first hired, I was tasked with making a list of open textbooks available online. I also found replacement materials that professors could use in courses. Over the course of a few months I made an Excel spreadsheet of 4,500 open textbooks available on the web, and this list is continually growing!

WHAT DID YOU LEARN AND WHAT SKILLS DID YOU ACQUIRE IN THE PROCESS?

As a student in information systems, learning HTML and CSS in my position were particularly useful as an introduction to programming before entering my actual programming courses. The tasks of my position allowed me to navigate the process of problem solving in a relatively risk-free environment. Conversely, my courses often introduced me to techniques and tools I could use in my position with open textbooks. For example, learning PHP in my programming course allowed me to edit a WordPress plugin to meet the unique needs of a particular programming textbook.

Troubleshooting design issues in my position introduced me to platforms such as Stack Overflow and GitHub, where I could interact with other contributors and find solutions to problems I came across. I was able to apply the solutions in one problem to a similar context in another problem, often with a creative and unique approach. These proved vital in my courses later on, where I would encounter more complex problems such as querying databases and creating UIs.

My position was also beneficial in the realm of project management. Working on a number of distinct textbooks with different needs, stakeholders, contributors, and deadlines improved my ability to estimate task times and switch back-and-forth between various tasks and requests. This was useful and applicable in my courses, where I had very different projects that demanded varying levels of attention. I needed to allocate my resources to succeed in my courses as efficiently as possible.

Researching open materials for my position in turn made me more adept at finding free learning resources to augment my own course materials. Where other students may have paid for supplementary course materials, I could find suitable free resources, saving me hundreds of dollars on my undergrad degree. Most students I encountered had no idea such materials existed.

WHAT DO YOU SEE AS PROCESSES OR PRACTICES THAT LEND THEMSELVES TO BEST SUCCESS WHEN FACULTY AND STUDENTS WORK ON THESE PROJECTS?

Communication is key when creating open textbooks. It's imperative that students (or any other contributors) understand the purpose and needs of the finished book. Everyone must be on the same page or there will be a lot of duplicate or superfluous work. Checking in with professors, faculty, and other student workers can ensure that nothing falls between the cracks. A task management system such as Basecamp or Asana may be useful to create project milestones and allocate work. This is more important as a team increases in size. Open Oregon State did not take full advantage of a task management system, but there were only about five student workers at any given time.

A cohesive "vision" for the department may help limit the scope of certain books that may require special attention (in my experience, these include math-based or programming books). This "vision" may need to develop over time and can include strategic intentions for both content and style. Since open textbook programs (and the open textbook industry in general) are relatively new for most universities, I believe this process is still in its infancy. A few standouts have emerged including BCcampus and the University of Minnesota. These are definitely models to follow for the establishment of new open textbook departments. I believe that OSU is emerging as an exemplary model.

It is imperative that the knowledge gained from student workers not be lost when they leave or graduate. There is a substantial learning curve that comes along with being hired in any position. Using previous student workers' perspectives and experiences to train new hires can not only speed up book production, but create a more cohesive body of work and culture within the department. I cannot stress enough how important I believe this legacy knowledge is.

Fostering a collaborative and open environment is vital for student workers to thrive and find creative solutions to complex problems. Create a space where students can work together and share input; this keeps them motivated and engaged when design work gets tedious. I was lucky to have a patient and open boss at Open Oregon State who listened to my ideas and considered my advice when making decisions. I would suggest that other open textbook department heads do the same: consider the opinions of your students workers. They have the perspective of both a student and a faculty member.

WHAT ARE SOME KEY CHALLENGES AND CONSIDERATIONS YOU WOULD LIKE TO SEE ADDRESSED IN SUCH PROJECTS?

For professors generously contributing content to open textbooks, they must be made aware of the limitations that certain platforms may have. For example, an HTML environment will not have the same cross-referencing or indexing capabilities as a LaTeX environment will. Illuminating these limitations from the start will prevent unnecessary work and avoid disappointment as the book progresses. However, the advantages and rewards of an open book must be emphasized over any potential shortcomings that may present themselves.

The interactivity and availability of supplementary materials must increase as more textbooks are developed. I believe this is one of the main hesitancies of professors in adopting an open textbook for their course. As the trust in open materials gains momentum over time, ability to replace existing materials in courses with minimal effort and exceeded expectations will prove to be essential.

ANYTHING ELSE YOU'D LIKE TO ADD?

Students' input is most essential, but can often be overlooked! I would like to see more projects emerge that aim to share the best practices of student workers, both within and across universities.

I would like to thank the Director of Open Oregon State Dianna Fisher for giving me the opportunity to learn and grow in this position. Her guidance, support, and willingness to allow me to take on new challenges provided a fulfilling environment for my first job.

CHAPTER 8

ADAPTING AN OPEN TEXTBOOK

In addition to creating open textbooks from scratch, some faculty and their students are working to adapt and remix or expand on existing open textbooks. Some notable examples follow.

Chapter 9

CASE STUDY: PRINCIPLES OF MICROECONOMICS

ED. ELIZABETH MAYS

Maxwell Nicholson's interest in open textbooks started as a student leader at the University of Victoria Students' Society.

He ran on a platform of open textbooks, and won (when we spoke with him he was just ending his post as director of campaigns and community relations). His involvement in an open textbook was one way of fulfilling a campaign promise to bring free textbooks into use at the university.

After the campaign, Nicholson met with about ten professors in exploratory meetings to find out about the barriers to adoption for open textbooks. These included Dr. Emma Hutchinson, who taught the ECON 103 course that Nicholson (and three of the other candidates) had been longtime lab instructors for.

"It's not going to go anywhere if the professor's not onboard, so we were fortunate enough for Dr. Hutchinson to be really excited about it too," Nicholson says.

Post-election, Nicholson's first step to operationalize the project was to apply for a $4,800 grant for the project from BC Campus, which served as a granting agency for open textbook projects that could prove a demand. Despite a few bumps along the way, the funds came through for the project.

This open textbook project was different in that rather than being primarily the work of an instructor with funding to write it or a class-assigned project for students, the grant funded lab instructors to do the heavy lifting of compiling the textbook. The professor reviewed it and made the changes they thought necessary from there. This was doable since Nicholson had direct experience with how the instructor taught the class.

Nicholson had assisted the microeconomics class three times and the macroeconomics course once. "I've been fortunate to be on the pedagogy side to some extent, obviously nothing compared to professors, but when writing the textbook, that was really really crucial for me to have that lens when I was contributing."

The textbook started as an adaptation of Timothy Taylor's open textbook, Principles of Microeconomics,[1] from OpenStax. But in the process of adapting the text, they found there were a lot of components that had to be written.

Ultimately, the textbook comprised around 30 percent material that came from Timothy Taylor's book and 70 percent new content the lab instructors developed from their notes and the professor's slide decks.

"The reason this project was most appealing is because she had her slides over here which taught what she wanted [students] to know, and then the publisher's textbook was completely different," NIcholson says. "So from the start our goal was really to align those two things."

Nicholson says the lab instructors thought a lot about how students were going to consume the material, and what components of the course the instructor really wanted to stress.

---

1. Timothy Taylor, *Principles of Microeconomics* (Houston, OpenStax: 2014), https://openstax.org/details/books/principles-microeconomics.

They hoped to save students the cost of buying a textbook they didn't really use.

The book was structured into eight topics, then the lab instructors divided them and did the heavy lifting to compile the chapters. Dr. Hutchinson edited each of the chapters to make sure everything was accurate, thorough and clear.

The process, Nicholson says, helped "remove the biggest barrier for professors–the magnitude of work that goes into redesigning a textbook."

Nicholson says he thinks large first-year courses such as ECON 103 (which has 800 students per year) make the best candidates for OER–and are also the most likely courses to have lab instructors that can be leveraged to compile the content. (He recognizes that most professors probably don't want to spend their nights and weekends becoming book publishers.)

"What [professors] can do if they know that they're going to do this project, is take one of their most christened lab instructors, get access to grant funding and pay the lab instructor to work on the textbook," Nicholson says. "Then they can be confident that it's someone who not only knows the course, but knows the course as the professor teaches it."

For his part, Nicholson says he learned a lot from the project, including understanding the work that goes into designing a course, and gaining a greater appreciation for good textbooks and discernment of those that aren't well-matched for the subject. Creating OER offers great opportunities to customize a textbook to a course, he says, observing that it must be challenging for traditional publishers to create one-size-fits-all content for teachers, who may teach subjects very differently.

"I would hope they're doing a lot of getting students to read this book and connect on it," he says. "A lot of times it feels like they don't."

Nicholson, who is studying business and economics, says, "If you're trying to create a product, you're always supposed to ask your end user 'what do you think?'"

So even if you don't want to have students write a textbook for your class, he says, you should have some of your top students read it and provide feedback.

Otherwise, he says, students will either buy the textbook and not use it, or tell future students not to buy it.

"With a publisher's resource, if it's not useful, the students are going to stop buying it," Nicholson says.

Of course, some might object to students having as much involvement in a textbook's writing as Nicholson and his fellow lab instructors experienced, but Nicholson says that after the instructors create the chapters, the professor is going to change and edit things, and ensure the quality meets their standard.

"If you're a respected faculty and you have the experience teaching and you've put that stamp of approval, I'm really confident that the resource is going to be [Dr. Hutchinson's] resource. It's not just some resource that was written by students."

For students involved in such projects, he encourages them to appreciate the potential impact they might have through their involvement.

"If you're involved in this kind of project, you're going to be on the back end of the course design, and you're able to take all the components that you thought were really bad about other textbooks and avoid those and leave all the really good elements," Nicholson says.

Students working on an open textbook for a class should realize the impact they'll have on future students who take that class–whether it's the only survey course they ever take on the subject, or the foundation of many in their majors. Plus, they're participating in an innovative movement in education.

Even for those who may not participate on an open textbook project, Nicholson says they can play a role in the movement as advocates, speaking with professors and outlining the benefits of OER, telling them when their book is expensive and there's an alternative open textbook in use by a peer institution.

"Creating the buzz about [open textbooks]–students can do that."

KEY TAKEAWAYS

For Faculty:

- Engage with student governments, who may be able to spread the word about your project and help recruit interested and willing students.
- Involve TAs who have both taken the course and are assisting in teaching the course and leverage their experience as students.
- Review existing materials (slide presentations, lesson plans, assignments and more) to see if there are any that can be converted into content for the open textbook.
- Get student feedback on the completed book. It's valuable! Be sure to implement fixes where appropriate for future editions.

For Students:

- Look for internal and external funding opportunities that may pay for your professor to hire you to help them create OER.
- Clarify roles, expectations, workflow, and timelines.

Chapter 10

CASE STUDY: EXPANDING THE OPEN ANTHOLOGY OF EARLIER AMERICAN LITERATURE

TIMOTHY ROBBINS, ASSISTANT PROFESSOR OF ENGLISH AT GRACELAND UNIVERSITY

OER, OPEN PEDAGOGY, AND THE EARLY AMERICAN LITERATURE SURVEY

At the start of each semester, I write a simple maxim on the board for discussion: "All people are equally intelligent." The underlying claim, in a paraphrased line from radical philosopher Jacques Rancière, is that any measurable differences in "intelligence" have more to do with access than with intellect. So, before course themes, content, objectives, or outcomes, I insist upon equality as a first principle and a constant practice. Then, as a group, we deliberate: what does "equal" mean in this context? How about "intelligent"? Is the claim true? How does it call upon us to relate to one another? Before the hour is up, we find ourselves in a thick of pedagogical inquiry, from which students tend to reach a fragile but thoughtful consensus: There really exists no one-size-fits-all measure for intelligence. Furthermore, the acquisition of knowledge assumed to be the epitome of individual intelligence–the "Jeopardy contestant" theory of smarts, as one student called it–is a tragic misconception. Learning, instead, is a collaborative enterprise: it's dialogic, responsive and revisable according to new information, and applicable to our everyday experience. So, yes, all people are in fact equally intelligent once we define "intelligence" more aptly as lived experimentation, rather than the highest grades and test scores.

I'm very clear with my students from the start: I wholeheartedly believe and affirm this principle. It's that very faith which prompted me to take up the ambitious Open Anthology project described below. And now I hope to build on that text and the pedagogical practices it demands for the rest of my scholarly career.

TEACHING A SURVEY OF "EARLY AMERICAN LITERATURE"

Two years ago, I was fortunate to be hired out right of graduate school and onto the tenure track as an "Early Americanist." All that means, effectively, is that, every year for the foreseeable future, I'll be teaching the English Department survey course titled "American Literature to 1900." That covers the period ranging from colonial contact with the "New World" (the world "new" to Europeans, that is) to the United States' industrial era, i.e., the beginnings of America's ascension to a global power.

I'll go on the record and say it's impossible to adequately cover any four centuries of literary history. But the truth is, I—newbie I was—made the task all the more impossible. For here I was, freshly trained in literary studies, newly recovering from the discipline's foundational urge to "cover" everything. My students, of course, would read deeply within and widely across the tradition's most celebrated authors. At the same time, it was my sacred duty to introduce the significant works of literature recovered since the explosion of "canon" in the last four to five decades. That includes the ever-growing roster of prose, poetry, and drama written by women, indigenous peoples, Africans and African-Americans, South American and Latinx authors, and ethnic immigrants.

So I went to work composing a reading list that could combine (or in the very least mediate) these opposing impulses. As a student of social movements, I like to adopt social history as a methodology, and so I saw "American Literature to 1900" as an opportunity to chart the various and contentious stories of the culture's movements towards emancipation and equality. As "America" was made into European colonies and eventually a liberal (white, patriarchal, landowner) democracy, from a country of farms and frontiers into an industrialized economic and military power, its literature played an important role in expanding the reading public and creating the definition of a nation. The course tracked roughly chronologically and featured the representative authors and texts. Indigenous creation stories confronted European colonial documents; the early texts of New England's Puritan pulpits were met and challenged by the voices and pens of native peoples, African slaves, and women writers. The American Revolution gave way to an explosion of social movements and an expansion of the canon stretching from Thomas Paine's republican propaganda to the birth of African-American letters in Phillis Wheatley. The selections from the early nineteenth century included the familiar names of the "American Renaissance" — Emerson, Poe, Hawthorne, Whitman, Melville — in tandem with the literature of women's rights and abolitionism. The final post-Civil War push balanced the social writings of the Gilded Age and Reconstruction with the co-emergence of realist fiction.

This literary historical narrative will seem familiar to Early American scholars, as will the course structure and the palpable tension it produced between content covered and time allowed. What was never at issue, for me, was locating a textbook. See, the literature survey course sports its own special media, the anthology; nearly exhaustive, this master text's pedagogical significance is matched only by its physical mass. The leading Early American anthologies on the academic market, — Wiley's *The Literatures of Colonial America*[1] and Norton's *Anthology of American Literature*[2] — are the size of small encyclopedias, coming in at 602 and 1845 pages, respectively. These truly impressive scholarly books,

---

1. Susan Castillo, and Ivy Schweitzer, eds. *The Literatures of Colonial America*, (Wiley: 2001), http://www.wiley.com/WileyCDA/WileyTitle/productCd-063121125X.html.

which introduced me and the current crop of Early American scholars to the field, have done a great deal in shaping our syllabuses and lesson plans, and, as a consequence, our conception of the era's literary output. That's not necessarily a bad thing. Again, these anthologies are excellent, compiled and edited by leading scholars in the field–all acquainted and attentive to the concerns of teaching the literature survey course.

That first fall semester, I decided to assign the Norton edition, chiefly because it contains Mark Twain's Adventures of Huckleberry Finn in its entirety. I figured a classic piece of fiction, one that allowed us to approach the fault lines between race, slavery, Reconstruction, and national identity, would make for a brilliant capstone. Yet for all of its helpful background material, framed by the anthology's wonderfully generative thematic groupings, our class never truly used the book. Admittedly, that's due in part to the sizable number of students who never even laid hands on it. The latest edition of the Norton American literature anthology retails at $81.25 to purchase and between $16 to $25 for a six-month rental. For many working-class, first-generation students, the costs of the text–or, the means to access it, a credit card, for example–are simply prohibitive. As a result, just two or three students bought the latest edition outright—though, they were all generous enough to share with friends. Some purchased older, used versions from online booksellers; still more relied on the web versions of assigned readings that I'd linked to on the course site.

The ensuing scramble and unevenness of our discussions proved a semester-long irritant. The medium was always the message. The few students who purchased the text had access to all the introductory material and paratextual supplements Norton offered. The rest had different editions with different page numbers, or online texts without page numbers; all seemed to be missing crucial excerpts at some point in the term. While a hand-

---

2. Nina Baym, et al., *The Norton Anthology of American Literature*, (W.W. Norton & Company, Inc.: 2011), http://books.wwnorton.com/books/detail.aspx?ID=23664.

ful of students read along in physical texts during class discussion, others multitasked on laptops or squinted through smartphone screen readings; still others, lacking any portable device, simply stared at the front of the room. It was a logistical nightmare of my own doing because, let's face it, the college anthology has one real utility and aim: to centralize all course content in an edited and professional manner ready to be taught. That is its appeal. The problem here was that, at the same time, the anthology was making some assumptions about our students, not just in its hefty price tag, but in its very centralizing and authoritative structure.

All the anthology had done for us at this point, where half the class hadn't adopted it, was allow me to dictate the content of "American Literature to 1900," raising "coverage" of authors and texts to supreme importance. To "learn" the period's literature, then, was to consume a whole bunch of texts, be they found in a fresh, glossy, weighty anthology or retrieved as HTML code on one's screen of choice.

OPEN EDUCATIONAL RESOURCES AND THE LITERATURE ANTHOLOGY

Right away, I decided I would scrap the paperback anthology the following fall, but I wavered on an alternative outside of simply posting a syllabus of hyperlinks on the site and providing introductory context through mini-lectures. Wasn't that just "banking education" for the digital age?

In the waning months of graduate school, — when I should have been writing — I began reading up on the burgeoning discussion around Open Educational Resources (OER), materials made free and available on the web to be accessed, downloaded, revised, and recirculated. The conversations of OER had already evolved beyond advocacy for their adoption as learning content, moving instead to sketch the larger contours of Open Education as a pedagogical principle. Recent studies–like the Florida Virtual Campus's annual surveys[3] –underscore that the integration of free and open textbooks cut costs, increase access, and improve student learning. Still, over and above replacing expensive industry textbooks, OER proponents contemplate how the virtues inherent to open materials necessitate new kinds of teaching and learning, methods that embrace the open ethos to reuse, remix, revise, and redistribute in content and practice. David Wiley, for example, has challenged[4] instructors to discard the "disposable" individual assignment in favor of collaborative and "renewable" open projects. Gardner Campbell recently called[5] for an Open Pedagogy centered on producing insight, where educators turn design over to students, encouraging them to take responsibility for their own learning. The discourse spoke to me.

In line with its disciplinary history, literary studies found itself at the forefront of open initiatives. Thus, after just a few weeks spent revisiting conversations around #openped, I discovered Robin DeRosa's rather heroic "open anthology," a text she created together with her Early American Literature students at Plymouth State. The project entailed that students read widely through the Early American syllabus and decide collectively which authors to excerpt and provide contextual materials for, before polishing and collecting their works in an online anthology to be read and revised by the following crop of students. Drawing on the legacy of Paulo Freire, DeRosa described[6] the project in more detail:

The open textbook allowed for student contribution to the "master text" of the course, which seemed to change the whole

---

3. "2016 Student Textbook and Course Materials Survey," *Florida Virtual Campus*, October 7, 2016, http://www.openaccesstextbooks.org/pdf/2016_Florida_Student_Textbook_Survey.pdf.
4. David Wiley, "What is Open Pedagogy," *iterating toward openness*, October 21, 2013, https://opencontent.org/blog/archives/2975.
5. Gardner Campbell, "2017: Quarks, Love and Insight," Gardner Campbell's professional website, January 1, 2017, http://www.gardnercampbell.net/blog1/?p=2603
6. Robin DeRosa, "My Open Textbook: Pedagogy and Practice," Robin DeRosa's professional website, May 18, 2016, http://robinderosa.net/uncategorized/my-open-textbook-pedagogy-and-practice/.

dynamic of the course from a banking model (I download info from the textbook into their brains) to an inquiry-based model (they converse with me and with the text, altering both my thinking and the text itself with their contributions).

The more I learned of the project, the more I liked it; and so, in true Open Pedagogy fashion, I stole it to redesign my own course.

Adopting the user-friendly Pressbooks[7] software, DeRosa and her students had managed to put together a promising framework for the "master text" in just a semester's time, what became the *Open Anthology of Earlier American Literature*.[8] As I reimagined the survey, following their lead and content, I saw that my inclination towards social history would be easy enough to retain. So, in the first half of our most recent iteration of "American Literature to 1900," we read through the texts published in the extant Pressbooks anthology–which included a potpourri of canonical and "minor" writers–interspersed with selections from some of the more conspicuously absent names, including Roger Williams, James Fenimore Cooper, William Apess, Ralph Waldo Emerson, and Margaret Fuller. Throughout the term, students agreed to complete short reading engagement worksheets, designed to both guide our in-class discussion and provide "training" in the editing skills needed to build out the anthology. In the latter half, we shifted focus to the hands-on project of remaking the anthology. We dedicated the final months to reading and discussing Open Education and Creative Commons licensing, learning the software, and practicing plenty on putting together materials for the various elements of the anthology—editing texts, locating and annotating biographical and secondary research, writing introductions, developing supplementary materials, and deliberating on how to make the texts "teachable." Teams of three built entries for authors and texts not yet represented, and, in the final

---

7. Pressbooks, https://pressbooks.com/.
8. Robin DeRosa, *The Open Anthology of Earlier American Literature* (Public Commons Publishing: 2015). https://openamlit.pressbooks.com/.

weeks of the term, led a classroom lesson based on their newly designed anthology chapter.

Truth be told, the analytical skills on display above are the same honed in any upper-level literature course, and they're assessed through similar assignments: regular reading and discussion, oral presentations, secondary research, critical source annotation, literature reviews, etc. The core difference came in the final product, and here there is, I think, a significant distinction. The traditional boss-level challenge in an English course is the literary critical essay, i.e., it is the peer-reviewed journal article in miniature—only in a version read and peer-reviewed by just one expert, the professor. Don't get me wrong, I still assign essays and I believe there's much to be gained from the craft, especially in terms of sharpening argumentation. But I think most literature instructors will confess to the assignment's utter "disposability," which is to say, while the skills developed and assessed in essay writing should endure over the course of a student's college career–and hopefully throughout their life–the actual assignment almost certainly will not. For her, the essay dies mercifully at the professor's desk, resurrected momentarily only as a final grade is uploaded to the registrar's website. That abrupt conclusion couldn't be more at odds with the intellectual afterlife of the professional essay, where publication at least aspires to respond and further instigate critical dialogue.

At its best, then, an "open" project like the student-designed anthology should simulate those aspects of intellectual collaboration and growth. Nowhere is that connection more apparent than in the project's demand for assessment. In our course, each group met with me to negotiate a grading contract that addressed the entire scope of their chapter, complete with an outline of group members' roles and workload and criteria for evaluation and grading. The practice forced students to take a kind of critical ownership of the project by thinking both proactively and reflectively on their own learning and engagement.

SOME PRACTICAL ADVICE

Dear reader, if by now you count yourself among the Open Anthology-converted, perhaps you're curious still about the finer details that go into re-organizing a survey course around an OER project. I leave you with a few tidbits of wisdom from my experience–including a sample syllabus and assignments, all of which you are welcome to steal (I mean, retain, reuse, revise, remix, and redistribute)[9] for your own course.

"SYLLABUS DAY"

- Because I have a flair for the dramatic, on day one I lugged the six or seven literature anthologies I own–all adorned with big, bright retail price tags–into class; I then heaved them onto a desk in the front of the room before launching into some ice breakers and then general introductions.

- Once the energy in the room felt upbeat and conducive to dialogue, I passed the tomes around and asked students to flip through the pages and mark down any familiar names and discernible thematic patterns across the texts. This is to provide a sense of the way scholars have conceptualized "Early American Literature."

- I then explained that we wouldn't, in fact, be using any of these books, but creating our own instead! That's when I introduced the existing Pressbooks anthology, the final project, and the concept of OER.

- I handed out a schedule with abbreviated course and assignment descriptions to be read for the next session.

TECHNOLOGY

Unless you can ensure that each student has personal access to

---

9. "Defining the 'Open' in Open Content and Open Educational Resources," *Opencontent.org*, http://www.opencontent.org/definition/.

a device–smartphones alone won't cut it, unfortunately–you will need to get into a computer lab at multiple points in the term.

- Pro tip: Reserve lab space early in the semester, preferably before it even begins. I went ahead and blocked out a room for the final month to help "train" students in Pressbooks (the software they would use to expand the anthology).
- Securing this space right away is especially important if your institution, like mine, is small and has limited tech resources on campus.

I am a great believer in the power of persistent and collaborative note taking.

- A class-wide or group-specific Google Doc[10] will still get the job done in this regard. In last year's class, I posted sparsely outlined "Keywords" and "Timeline" Google Docs to the course site and had students develop them via in-class and homework assignments throughout the term.
- For in-text highlighting and notes, I use the annotation tool Hypothesis.is, a web overlay that is not only easy to use[11] in the classroom, but is tailor-made for groupwork[12] tasks and for use in Pressbooks.[13]
- The most important aspect of these tools–and, I would argue, of any you choose to introduce in the course–is that students can be given the option to publish

---

10. Shep McAllister, "Use Google Docs to Collaborate on Class Note Taking," *Huffington Post*, http://www.huffingtonpost.com/hack-college/use-google-docs-to-collab_b_844192.html.
11. "Quick Start Guide for Teachers," *Hypothes.is*, https://web.hypothes.is/quick-start-guide/.
12. "Creating Groups," Hypothes.is, https://web.hypothes.is/creating-groups/.
13. Zoe Wake Hyde, "Introducing: Hypothesis Annotations in Pressbooks," *Pressbooks*, https://pressbooks.com/blog/introducing-hypothesis-annotations-in-pressbooks/.

- privately among peers or anonymously with a private nod to the instructor.
- Last, I think it is important to give students the option of adopting "lo-tech" methods, too–i.e., note taking with machine-made pen and paper–as a substitute to the abovementioned.

As far as expanding, revising, and publishing a scholarly anthology via Pressbooks, Julie Ward has written a fabulous primer for chapter fifteen of this very handbook.[14]

ASSIGNMENTS

If you're looking to reproduce this project to expand Robin DeRosa's American Literature anthology, but you need broad ideas on the course schedule and structure, and/or specific tasks to accompany the readings, and/or a general set of guidelines for the final project, I give to you my initial crack at a syllabus (Attachment A[15]), sample "reading guides" (Attachments B,[16] C,[17] D,[18] and E[19]), and a final project assignment sheet (Attachment F[20]).

Note: The "reading guides" (Attachments B-E) are effectively daily homework assignments that are to be peer-reviewed in class. Intended as scaffolding tasks to introduce students to Early American authors and texts, reading guides should also progressively build on the concepts and skills needed to curate anthology chapters in the latter part of the course while also helping

---

14. Julie Ward, "Teaching Assignment: Expand an Open Textbook," *Guide to Making Open Textbooks With Students,* https://press.rebus.community/makingopentextbookswithstudents/chapter/teaching-assignment-expand-an-open-textbook/.
15. Timothy Robbins, "Open Early American Literature Syllabus," http://bit.ly/2AhrYyh
16. Timothy Robbins, "William Bradford Reading Guide," http://bit.ly/2jzEo1r
17. Timothy Robbins, "James Fenimore Cooper Reading Guide," http://bit.ly/2kpF8m4
18. Timothy Robbins, "Nathaniel Hawthorne Reading Guide," http://bit.ly/2AgcA54
19. Timothy Robbins, "Open American Literature Anthology Reading Guide," http://bit.ly/2APZsVi
20. Timothy Robbins, "American Literature to 1900 Final Project," http://bit.ly/2yirg1L

students connect (what's more than likely to be) foreign material–colonial documents, oral tales, Puritan sermons, etc.–to contemporary issues that seem more relevant to their everyday experiences.

> **KEY TAKEAWAYS**
>
> - Build on an existing open textbook to expand it.
> - Get your students to reflect on their participation and engagement in the collaborative project. Ask them to develop their own grading rubrics, outline individual and group roles, or more.
> - Think about how you can add to the "traditional" approach to your subject matter to engage students and how an open textbook might afford those opportunities.
> - Frame learning as an ongoing process rather than one that ends upon receipt of a final grade.

Timothy Robbins *is an assistant professor of English at Graceland University. His research interests include literature of the "Long Nineteenth Century" in the United States, especially the poetry and prose of Walt Whitman, as well as protest literature and reception theory.*

CHAPTER 11

STUDENT SPOTLIGHT: MATTHEW MOORE, THE OPEN ANTHOLOGY OF EARLIER AMERICAN LITERATURE, 2ND EDITION

MATTHEW MOORE, ENGLISH AND STUDIO ART MAJOR AT GRACELAND UNIVERSITY

was among the students who worked on professor Tim Robbins' classroom project at Graceland University to expand *The Open Anthology of Earlier American Literature*. Enrolled in Tim's Early American Literature course last fall, he introduced an assignment that would entail us contributing and expanding an open anthology of literature. Most of us must have pondered: "open anthology"? I know I did. Divided into groups, each of us took on various roles from writing introductions for literary works to researching biographical information to provide brief historical context. Although initially daunting, I don't think I speak only for myself when I say that as a class this assignment offered rewards and payoffs both intellectually and communally; plus, it was just plain fun. My group in particular chose the works of Roger Williams to curate, write introductions to, and research Williams' historical impact. Here, I quickly realized the importance of such an anthology. Williams' work fought in defense of indigenous people's rights in North America. Neither I nor the rest of my group had encountered his works or narratives in high school classes.

It became clear that this was more than just some group project reinforcing the value of collaboration or how to conduct proper research; the open source anthology plugged a handful of university undergraduates into a larger, reciprocal community between peers and instructors. Ultimately, however, that line began to blur. The autonomy and authority fostered in the students, and the fact that this project actively sought and utilized student perspectives, was empowering. Engaged with this digital pedagogy, given backstage passes to the world of academic anthologies, we curated works that seemed urgent for a new generation of students. In this way, it was our own critique of the traditional and reiterated canon that has been burnt into the retinas of undergrad English majors anywhere. Within that space we included untold histories, suppressed narratives, and stories that didn't make the cut. In a small yet surprisingly diverse university with students from all different cultural and ethnic backgrounds and who encounter literature in their own nuanced ways, the inclusion of these pieces was vital. It was less a matter of reprinting a time-honored magnum opus as it was a cultural responsibility to validate the works of quelled voices.

We also, indirectly, became acquainted with the bureaucratic side of anthologizing: working within open domain and the restrictions of copyright, which lent insight into the inner workings of the literary industry.

It dawned on me: in the larger picture, and with each contribution, we were opening access to academic material to a global community; possibly even to some without access to higher education. In that sense, we felt as if our positions of academic privilege, in this case, were used in a productive and egalitarian way, even if it may have been a small feat. Knowing that our contributions to the open source anthology would be read, understood, and interpreted by future readers from all avenues of life is a mesmerizing thought.

Having been led to believe in the authoritative role of the textbook, its glorified place in academia, this project turned that notion on its head and, instead, cultivated a community of student-to-student communication that was far more productive and valuable to some of us than purchasing a $150 textbook. From the university student who can't afford the textbook, let alone grip the thing, to the literary nerd aimlessly scouring the recesses of the Internet in search of a literary text, the benefits of being open are many. With an anthology for students written by students, we break away from a precedent of reading these works in esoteric circles, and open new, inclusive frontiers of engaging with a text and, more important, having access to it.

> **KEY TAKEAWAYS**
>
> - Bring in different perspectives from faculty and students while working on the project. In so doing, empower your students by placing their feedback on par with faculty reviews.

Matthew Moore *is an English and studio art major at Graceland University.*

PART III

STUDENT RIGHTS & FACULTY RESPONSIBILITIES

When making open textbooks with students, faculty have a responsibility to keep student rights front of mind. Privacy, licensing, and digital literacy are among the main issues to consider.

CHAPTER 12

LICENSING

Practitioners of Open Pedagogy generally recommend that students have agency in their choice of license for a class project. This means they should be educated on the nuances of the license and what that means for how their work can be used in the future. In addition, they should have a choice in the matter of which license is selected. And that choice should not impact their ability to complete the assignment for class credit.

> **LICENSING ISSUES FOR CONTENT CREATED IN CLASS PROJECTS**
>
> Key questions to consider:
>
> - Can students in your class project choose whether to openly license their work or not?
> - What implications might this have for the usability of the completed work?
> - If they do choose an open license, can they choose which license to use?
> - If they choose a restrictive license, will their contributions still be part of the finished book?
> - Do all the students have to come to consensus, or can they choose the license for their individual

> contributions? What is the decision process when there are small-group contributions?
>
> - How do students want to be cited and attributed in their work and future derivatives?
> - What if they do not want to be cited at all and prefer to be anonymous or keep their work private?
> - How can students use the work in their portfolios or professional websites, if desired?
> - How will you take advantage of this topic to teach digital literacy to students around the concept of openness?

In a recent event at Rebus Community, we spoke with Robin DeRosa, chair of interdisciplinary studies at Plymouth State University, Steel Wagstaff, instructional technology consultant at UW-Madison, and Amanda Coolidge, senior manager of Open Education at BCcampus, about their experiences working with students to create open textbooks

The three talked about pedagogy, faculty responsibilities, student rights, and agreements when students work on open textbooks and OER projects.

One of the key threads that emerged was the need for students to have agency over their choice of license–meaning they're not forced into an open license without understanding what it is, and the alternatives.

Robin said she handles this by giving her students choices: They can choose whether to openly license their work or not, and if they do choose an open license, they can choose which license to use. (But if their chosen license is not compatible with the other licenses, their contributions may not get into the finished book, she said, citing the more restrictive CC ND license as one example.)

Robin said over the three courses in which she has focused on open, she has only had one student keep their coursework fully private inside the LMS.

"I don't think there's any problem giving them all of that choice. It only works to reinforce the Open Pedagogy, which is that you are in the driver's seat and you have control over what you do," she said.

Steel also mentioned the students' intellectual property rights (i.e. copyright) to what they create.

"In part I think Open Pedagogy is empowering them to say, 'hey this is your content. What do you want to do with it?'" Steel said.

When publishing an openly licensed book, he said, "our strategy was that we wanted to obtain consensus on the license."

He also talked with students about the attribution component of the license and encouraged students to think about how they wanted their work to be cited and attributed.

Steel noted that students should be able to choose not to use the open license and still get credit for the course and meet its educational goals.

Amanda said Open Pedagogy provides a great opportunity to teach digital literacy to students around the concept of openness.

"What does it mean to contribute back to the public good, and is that something you want to do or is that something you feel restricted by?"

> **KEY TAKEAWAYS**
>
> - Get a librarian to talk to your students about the various types of licenses. You can read more in our Guide to Creative Commons licenses.
> - Conduct an exercise in which students can pick their own license.

CHAPTER 13

PRIVACY & ANONYMITY

Privacy is also a concern, both ethically and legally, when embarking on Open Pedagogy projects.

Robin says she handles this by offering her students the option to use a pseudonym.

"You might have people who want to be in the open but they don't want to develop their own digital identity attached to their real identity," Robin said. "But if you're going to allow that as an option you just have to understand enough about how privacy works on the web and data so that you're not offering them some false sense of privacy that isn't actually authentic."

Steel said he is conscious of the students' right to privacy under FERPA when building materials in the course of their education. He suggested several options to protect this federally mandated right of students.

1. Get FERPA waivers from the students.
2. Make the open resource and credit the students who contributed, but without identifying that they were part of a specific course.
3. Allow students to use pseudonyms when building the open resource.
4. All of the above.

He noted that not all students will feel personally passionate or attached to the things they build under their name in a course, and especially when projects are public, digital and archived in perpetuity on the web, they should not be forced to be affiliated with something they've done as classwork indefinitely.

David Squires, a visiting assistant professor teaching in Washington State University, who worked with his students to develop an OER textbook on social media, solved this attribution dilemma by crediting the students who built the open resource at the front of the book, rather than attaching individual students' names to the chapters they specifically worked on.

CHAPTER 14

DIGITAL LITERACY

DAVID SQUIRES

BETWEEN MAKING AND INTEGRATING DIGITAL TECHNOLOGY

Advocacy for digital literacy often falls along a spectrum from making to integrating computing technologies. We can see this tendency in the excitement over maker spaces and technology integration. Pedagogically, both have their value, as articulated in the representative statements from Educause and Edutopia:

> "Makerspaces allow students to take control of their own learning as they take ownership of projects they have not just designed but defined."[1]
> "Technology, when integrated into the curriculum, revolutionizes the learning process. More and more studies show that technology integration in the curriculum improves students' learning processes and outcomes."[2]

If maker spaces let students become better producers, technology integration lets them become savvier consumers. While maker spaces emphasize student agency and technical creativity, technology integration emphasizes student awareness and technical proficiency. Both, however, come with a high price tag, making

---

1. Educause Learning Initiative, "7 Things You Should Know about Makerspaces," *Educause*, https://net.educause.edu/ir/library/pdf/ELI7095.pdf.
2. "Why Do We Need Technology Integration?," *Edutopia*, November 5, 2007, https://www.edutopia.org/technology-integration-guide-importance.

them unfeasible options for many instructors. Creating Open Educational Resources (OERs) with students offers one possible synthesis for making and integrating at a scale that Paul Fyfe calls "mid-sized digital pedagogy."[3] Working with students on an open textbook promotes collaboration with affordable tools while also letting students stay focused on course content.

When students begin to produce open textbooks, they necessarily delve into the subject area of the course. The task demands at the outset a level of systematic thinking that course materials assume in advance. Textbook authors and college professors usually take responsibility for course design and so set the parameters for student learning. By contrast, creating open textbooks as a class project invites professors and students to enter into a collaborative process for deciding what content to feature and how to organize it. One of the most challenging—but also energizing—aspects of creating OERs in my experience came at the beginning of the project when students divided the chapter topics for a textbook on social media. They had to ask critical questions about what counts as comprehensive knowledge and how best to sequence learning from the fundamental to the more specialized. Before ever worrying about software for layout and publishing, students immersed themselves in the secondary literature and research materials. Importantly, they drew on previously published open textbooks where possible, which pushed the collaborative experience beyond the walls of our classroom to a wider academic community. Students realized quickly that they had a responsibility to both the authors who went before them and the readers who might use their textbook.

Because I teach digital cultural studies my courses can unify digital literacy instruction with course content, perhaps more than other subjects. For my purposes, having students create an open textbook on social media encouraged them to explore aspects of everyday culture that they often overlook. For instance, as a

---

3. Paul Fyfe, "Mid-Sized Digital Pedagogy," *Debates in the Digital Humanities* (University of Minnesota Press, 2016), http://dhdebates.gc.cuny.edu/debates/text/62.

class they decided that the textbook should include a chapter on the terms of service for using Facebook, Instagram, Twitter, and other popular social media platforms. That decision required them to study seemingly arcane details about computer fraud as well as details about their own (often eroded) rights as content creators. The section on copyright limitations echoed the discussions we had in advance about Creative Commons licensing and the various motivations underlying the move toward OERs. The exploration of terms of service left students with a new awareness for their own labor as content producers on platforms designed, in large part, for mass consumption. At the same time, writing textbook material let them reimagine their role in class as not simply knowledge consumers but also as knowledge producers. The goal of turning college students into knowledge producers is not unique to digital literacy curricula, of course, but digital literacy can help achieve that goal with a critical eye toward the broader context of content creation under commercially oriented copyright regimes.

Concerns over copyright and proprietary content extend to choosing a desktop publisher and distribution platform. Many of my students need to learn Adobe tools such as InDesign for professional reasons. Given the cultural studies focus on my courses, however, we picked a free, open source web application called Scalar. Scalar was designed to feature academic writing with media rich content. It lent itself to our textbook prototype because it works on the book model. As a digital tool, however, it also takes advantage of all that interactive media affords, including the ability to feature and annotate images, video, sound, maps, and almost any web-based material with a stable URL. That gives Scalar an advantage over PDF publications, which my students exploited to incorporate primary examples from around the web, especially YouTube, in their original form. Admittedly, Scalar creates a learning curve that some students find frustrating. For instance, the platform lets users add media by linking it to specific parts of the text, rather than just dropping it between paragraphs. Although more complex, the benefit of creating media links is that the written analysis has a direct relationship to the object of study, making critical reading skills manifest in the organization of digital content. The added complexity encourages students to work outside their comfort zone as they think about the relationship between digital media and their own writing.

As a platform, Scalar exemplifies the synthesis of making and integrating digital media. Students become publishers in the process of writing their Scalar book even as they practice integrating digital media from various web sources. The assignment works to develop comprehensive mastery over the course material while students also ask critical questions about which materials get selected for study and which get excluded. Similarly, they can ask which tools become the defaults for learning and which get marginalized. One of my students wondered aloud during in-class discussion why textbooks have become a dominant tool from primary to higher education. It's a good question, although not one we were able to answer in that class. Having asked, however, the student offered us an expanded sense of literacy that includes working with a wealth of media technologies in addition to reading books and writing papers.

That broad view of literacy needs full consideration in an age when we're faced with choosing among an endless number of applications to solve any given problem, especially when many of those applications will threaten our rights as content creators and our privacy as consumers.

PART IV

SAMPLE ASSIGNMENTS

Use these example assignment materials to create or expand an open textbook as an Open Pedagogy project in your classroom.

Chapter 15

Teaching Guide: Expand an Open Textbook

JULIE WARD, ASSISTANT PROFESSOR OF 20TH AND 21ST-CENTURY LATIN AMERICAN LITERATURE AT UNIVERSITY OF OKLAHOMA

Below is a teaching guide from Dr. Julie Ward at University of Oklahoma for instructors wishing to expand an existing open textbook project in their classes. While this project is specific to Spanish literature, the advice is relevant to similar projects in other disciplines.

CRITICAL EDITION ASSIGNMENT IMPLEMENTATION GUIDE

Welcome to the *Antología Abierta de Literatura Hispana (AALH)* team! I (Julie Ward) am so thrilled that you and your students will be participating in this enriching learning experience and providing materials for other students around the world.

This guide is a week-by-week overview of how I implemented the critical edition in my third-year university Spanish course, Introduction to Hispanic Literature and Culture. Feel free to use what is helpful and ignore what isn't. I do ask that if you plan to stray too far from the format here that you email me (wardjulie@ou.edu) so we can discuss how it will fit into the *AALH*.

You'll see that I dedicated seven class periods over ten weeks to the critical edition group project. It's an intensive research project that introduces many students to the concept of literary research for the first time, and I think you'll be very impressed at students' in-depth knowledge of their chosen texts and authors by the time they present their final products.

Good luck, and if you have any questions please don't hesitate to get in touch: wardjulie@ou.edu

WEEK 1: GROUP WORK, AN OVERVIEW

Time: 50 minutes
Objective: Discuss and reflect on group work; share best practices; create team expectations agreements.

Prior work for instructor:

- Set up groups of 4-5 students each (I highly recommend using CATME if possible; either way, see the best practices laid out in Oakley et al. section II.C, pp. 12-13, including *Getting to Know You Form* pp. 24-25).
- Make copies of "Coping with Hitchhikers and Couch Potatoes on Teams" (1/student, Oakley et al. pp. 33-34).
- Make copies of "Normas y expectativas del equipo de trabajo" (1/group, Appendix A).

Prior work for students:

- Read "What Google Learned on its Quest to Build the Perfect Team."
- Complete 5-question reading quiz (sample here).

In Class:

- Follow the script in Oakley et al., Section II.D-III.C, pp. 13-16.
- Have students read "Coping with Hitchhikers and Couch Potatoes on Teams" in Oakley et al. pp. 33-34 in their groups and discuss the following questions:

- What is your overall opinion of group work in classes?
- What was the worst group-work experience you've ever had? What made it difficult?
- What was the best group-work experience you've ever had? What was great about it?

- Elicit responses from students as a group.
- Acknowledge possible difficulties with group work and discuss the strategies you will implement to address them proactively.
- Go over Team Policies (Oakley et al. p. 26 or see Appendix A for version in Spanish).
- Have each group write its Team Expectations Agreement and turn in a copy, signed by all members, to you (Oakley et al. pp. 26-27 or see Appendix A for version in Spanish).
- Announce dates for 1) reforming groups (optional); 2) team evaluations.
- Explain how team evaluations will affect project grade for individuals.

WEEK 2: WHAT IS A SCHOLARLY EDITION?

Time: 50 minutes
Objective: Define scholarly edition; introduce assignment.

Prior work for instructor:

- Bring several examples of critical editions of literary texts to class, at least one per student.
- Make copies of "Exploración de ediciones críticas" (Appendix B) (1/student).
- Bring copies (or project on screen) of Critical Edition

Assignment Sheet and Ejemplo Formato Edición Crítica.

Prior work for students:

- Read "MLA Statement on the Scholarly Edition in the Digital Age."
- Complete comprehension quiz "Ediciones críticas" over reading (sample here).

In Class:

- Elicit preliminary definitions of a critical or scholarly edition.
- Pass out one or two critical editions to each group along with "Exploración de ediciones críticas" worksheet.
- Ask students to use the critical editions to answer the questions on the worksheet.
- When students have completed worksheets, have each group share their responses, presenting their selected edition to the class.
- If necessary, revise preliminary definitions of critical and scholarly editions.
- Explain that each group will be creating a smaller-scale version of the critical editions they just examined, by choosing one text studied in class this semester and writing an introduction, providing annotations, and including relevant illustrations and bibliography.
- Show students the *Antología abierta de literatura hispana* and explain that their completed, successful entries will form part of future editions of the *AALH*. Mention that students will license their entries CC-BY, to be discussed in Week 5.
- Pass out critical edition assignment sheet (Appendix C) and "Ejemplo Formato Edición Crítica" (Appendix D)

and present due dates and expectations, and answer questions.

WEEK 3: DETERMINE WORK

Each group should schedule a time to meet with the instructor and/or a TA during this week to choose a work for their critical edition. Students should be encouraged to look ahead at the syllabus and familiarize themselves with the options.

Any text chosen should be in the public domain or licensed CC-BY for inclusion in the *AALH*. There is a wish list of authors available here.

Only one group should work on a given text.

Schedule between 15-30 minutes per group.

WEEK 5: TEAM WORK ANALYSIS AND REVIEW PROCESS / CC-BY OVERVIEW

Time: 50 minutes
Objectives: Analyze team progress and review selves and teammates; Discuss best practices for providing feedback; Learn about Creative Commons licensing and sign MOU.

Prior work for instructor:

- Make copies of Oakley et al. pp. 28, 30 (1/student) and p. 29 (for each student, one per group member including themselves, i.e., 4-5/student).
- Bring sealable envelopes (1/student).
- Schedule Visit from on-campus specialist on Creative Commons Licensing, probably a digital resources librarian (if possible).
- Make copies of MOU from Rebus Community (Appendix E).

In class:

- "Hand out Evaluation of Progress toward Effective Team Functioning [(Oakley et al. p. 28)...] to get students to reflect on how their team is doing. Students are inclined to sweep problems under the rug until the problems become severe enough to cause explosions. Periodic reviews of what is going well and what needs work can get the problems on the table where they can be dealt with in a less emotional and more constructive manner. Again, other than handing out, collecting, and keeping the evaluations on file, the instructor normally would not comment or take action in response to them unless they suggest that an explosion is imminent (and perhaps not even then)" (Oakley et al. 16)
- "Have the students fill out Team Member Evaluation forms (Oakley et al., p. 29) for each team member (including themselves) and discuss them with one another" (Oakley et al. 17).
- "Have the students [...] summarize their verbal ratings on the Peer Rating of Team Members Form [Oakley et al. p. 30...], and submit the latter form into the instructor. A good idea is to have the students submit the forms in sealed envelopes, with the student team names or numbers on the outside— this makes it easy to sort the forms for each group" (Oakley et al. 18).
- Introduce librarian, who will explain public domain, what Creative Commons licensing is and what CC-BY licensing in particular is. Be sure to emphasize that students will be licensing their critical editions CC-BY and what the implications and motivations for this are. (For more information, see the Rebus Community Licensing FAQ.)
- Pass out MOU and ask each student to sign it and return it to you.

After class:

- "Use the autorating system [Oakley et al. p. 31 . . .] to convert the verbal ratings to numerical ones, calculate a weighting factor for each team member, and determine each student's individual grade as the product of the team assignment grade and the weighting factor for that student. This system is not shared with the students unless an individual student asks (in our experience, they almost never do). [. . . I]nstructors should reserve the right to disregard any ratings that look suspicious after attempting to understand the dynamics that produced them." (Oakley et al. 18) [NB: Decide how you want to incorporate peer ratings into your grading scheme.]

WEEK 7: CHECKLIST

Time: 25 minutes
Objectives: Reality Check on progress vis a vis upcoming due date.

Prior work for instructor:

- Print checklist (1/student) (Appendix G).

Prior work for students:

- Each group should bring, in digital or paper form, the current version of their critical edition.

In class:

- Give students a copy of the requirements checklist and ask them to fill it out according to their group's progress on the critical edition.
- Once students have assessed their progress, have them

make a plan and delegate tasks for finishing by the due date.

WEEK 9: PEER REVIEW

Time: 50 minutes
Objectives: Provide and receive feedback on critical edition for final revisions.

Prior work for instructor:

- Print peer review sheet (1/student) (Appendix G).

Prior work for students:

- Each group should bring 5-6 hard copies of their critical editions, one for the instructor and one for each member of the reviewing group.

In Class:

- Hand out peer review worksheet and go over questions with students. Elicit examples of helpful feedback and not-so-helpful feedback.
- Pair groups and have them exchange their critical editions. The peer review worksheet should be filled out individually by each group member.
- Give students approximately 20-25 minute to fill out the form.
- Have paired groups come together and give them 20 minutes (10 minutes/group) to share feedback with one another.
- Remind students of next week's due date/presentations.

WEEK 10: PRESENTATIONS

The presentation of the scholarly editions may take the form of timed group presentations, or of a poster session where students take turns staying with a monitor showing their digital critical edition and explaining it to others and visiting other groups' stations to see their work. You may find it helpful to pass out the evaluation form in Appendix H to guide students as they observe one another's work.

Additionally, you may offer a "Premio Popular" for whichever group receives the highest evaluations from peers.

If any university offices or departments, such as the office of undergraduate research or the libraries, helped you to implement this assignment, this is an excellent occasion to allow students to demonstrate their new expertise and for campus contacts to see the fruit of their labor.

*Don't forget to assign a final Peer and Self Evaluation (See Week 5 above) once the project is complete.

APPENDICES

Please follow the links below to the appendices:

- Appendix A: Normas y Expectativas del Equipo de Trabajo[1]
- Appendix B: Exploración de Ediciones Críticas[2]
- Appendix C: Critical Edition Assignment Sheet[3]
- Appendix D: Ejemplo del Formato de la Edición Crítica[4]
- Appendix E: Faculty/Student MOU[5]
- Appendix F: Checklist[6]

---

1. Julie Ward, "Critical Edition Assignment Implementation Guide," http://bit.ly/jwcriticaledgdoc.
2. Ibid.
3. Ibid.
4. Ibid.
5. Ibid.
6. Ibid.

- Appendix G: Peer Review[7]
- Appendix H: Evaluation Forms[8]

7. Ibid.
8. Ibid.

CHAPTER 16

ASSIGNMENT: CREATE AN OPEN TEXTBOOK

ANNA ANDRZEJEWSKI, ART HISTORY PROFESSOR AND DIRECTOR OF GRADUATE STUDIES AT THE UNIVERSITY OF WISCONSIN-MADISON

> *Below is an example of an open textbook creation project assigned by professor Anna Andrzejewski at University of Wisconsin. While this assignment is specific to Art History, it could easily be adapted to other disciplines and your own classroom learning objectives. Assignment #2 followed an earlier project in which each student focused on a phase of Frank Lloyd Wright's career (in time) or a theme in his work in order to build a chapter providing overall context. In this, part two of the assignment, students visited significant local Frank Lloyd Wright architectural landmarks and developed a chapter highlighting each of them.*

GROUP PROJECT ASSIGNMENT

BY ANNA ANDRZEJEWSKI

You have been assigned to work in a group one of Frank Lloyd Wright's (or his followers') buildings in Madison. Your "chapter" on your research on this building is the focus of this project. Also, you will want to revise your first group project assignment as well (see below) making suggested revisions offered by the Instructor earlier in the term. **Please read this carefully**; it contains much of what you need to know (though specific details of formatting – including for references and potentially image credits – will follow at a later date).

OBJECTIVE OF THE GROUP PROJECTS

Our class is collectively working on a "textbook" for future classes and the public on Frank Lloyd Wright's Madison buildings. The first group assignment (Group Project Assignment #1) was meant as a frame for Wright's career. Each group was to focus on a "phase" of Wright's career (in time) or a theme in his work, and the overall "chapter" – produced as a collective product of the class – thus is intended to provide a context for the chapters that follow (Group Project Assignment #2) – each of which deals with a building by Wright (or his followers) in Madison.

Given the goal of this project being a textbook for a generalist audience, this content should be easily producible – meaning, you have a good bit of information from our readings and site visits to write something pretty spiffy. I'm asking you to do a bit of additional research to enrich the chapter on your building and also make revisions to the portion of the first chapter (Group Project Assignment #1). That revision process is explained below.

Since this is a textbook, you also want to produce it in a way that is readable and approachable. You should use shorter sentences and clear and precise language. When appropriate, use images, movies, diagrams, maps to make your points. You can also use tables and callout boxes to amplify key points. This is an opportunity to be creative as well as scholarly! Have fun.

REVISIONS TO GROUP PROJECT ASSIGNMENT #1

As noted in the previous guidelines (Group Project Assignment #1), the goal of this was to provide a CONTEXT for your particular building. That can be through chronology (i.e., the "prairie phase") or through a theme (i.e., organic architecture). All groups did this relatively successfully, though as you write your CHAPTER (Group Assignment #2) you will likely want to add/change things in the introductory chapter. For example, you may find illustrations of other similar buildings you want to include in your original (GP #1) entry. Or you may realize you talked too much about your building in the first assignment and will want to move content from your first group project assignment to the second.

Although your grade on the first group project assignment will not change, you will be partly graded on the 2nd group project assignment on REVISING the first group project assignment. 20% of your grade for GROUP PROJECT ASSIGNMENT #2 is based on "cleaning up" your initial post. In addition to fine-tuning the content (responding to my feedback and suggestions and bringing it in line with the rest of the class), I would ask everyone to address the following in their revisions:

- Standardize the reference format to bring it in line with the standards for Group Project Assignment #2 (that may mean adding footnotes...required).
- Add images to make your entry visually appealing.
- Delete any text that is not relevant to your theme (basic facts about Wright's career or biography.

There is no standard length for these – some may be shorter or longer depending on the points you are trying to make. But they should be at least 2-3 paragraphs and perhaps longer.

GROUP PROJECT ASSIGNMENT #2

Your focus for the rest of term should be on producing content for the chapter on your building. You will be working with the same partner(s) on this. Please work together and plan ahead. I will give you suggestions on sources to look at and other information, but you should feel free to take this your own direction based on your individual interests and your group as a whole.

As noted above, you want to provide information that is of interest to future students as well as a general audience. To that end, your chapter has to include some basic information, a building description, and a more interpretive section (a three-part structure). The interpretive section is where the individual interest and the interest/focus of your group as a whole come in. The basic information and building description must be there, and they should be front and center in the chapter. To that end, I suggest dividing your chapter into sections.

1. **Introduction.** This should give *at minimum* the building name, building type (house, church, or other), date and location (and any other important information – i.e., Lamp House, you may want to note who it was built for (the patron)), and a statement of the thesis of the chapter – this is the *main point* you want to convey through the narrative. This should be 1-2 paragraphs long at most.
2. **Description.** Your description should give the reader a "mental picture" through narrative of what your building looks like. It should discuss (at least minimally) the following: size (including square footage, function and # of rooms) and height (# of stories, for example); materials (focusing on the main exterior materials, and interior ones as relevant); "style" (both in relation to the period in which it was built and in Wright's own body of work – i.e., prairie, usonian, or other). You should consider discussing layout as well – i.e., how the floor plan works. This section should be illustrated abundantly. Try to put in floor plans, historic photos, and current photos (as appropriate). Images should not replace narrative description; they should mutually reinforce one another. This section should be at least 3 paragraphs long, likely 4-5. Do not feel compelled to go "room by room" or "floor by floor." I will try to provide examples.
3. **Interpretive section.** Part 3 will be your "interpretive section." This should have a subheading appropriate to

what it is. It may simply be History of the X Building. Or it could be more thematic (i.e., The Lamp House as a Statement of Wright's Personal Ties to Madison). Here you want to showcase your "take" on the building. Use what interested you about it to make a POINT (or perhaps a FEW POINTS) about why it is interesting to you (to you individually and to your group as a whole). It should not be a series of random thoughts or a series of things you found in research sources; it should, rather, work toward a point (or several points). Here are some possible topics you could focus on for this:

- Patronage (how the building relates to the patron (the person for whom the building is built)
- Construction technology (example would be modular building or prefabrication)
- The relationship of the building to Wright's theories of architecture (i.e., art and craft of the machine, or perhaps organic building, or Usonia)
- The relationship of the building (and/or its patron) to Madison or its particular geographic context

To reiterate, this interpretive section can have more than one point, and it could address more than one of these categories (or even others not on this list). But it shouldn't be a series of random observations!

You want to show in this section you've "listened" to our class discussions at the sites as well as your classmates' feedback. I will send you summaries of what interested your classmates (from their journals). You also have access to the discussion boards. This information should not be quoted or used in your books but should be inspiration for your chapter's theme and its content.

You also want to show evidence of "research" here beyond the class. I will suggest books and other reference sources for you to consult. There are other resources you can look to as well – here are a few to consider. I would divvy these up and look at them, or consider them all (in one way or another).

- **Madcat/library book search.** Our library contains TONS of books on Frank Lloyd Wright and even on specific buildings, including these.
- **Avery Index of Architectural Periodicals.** This is a library networked database that contains articles on architectural history; you can search Wright and your building (by its various names) in it.
- **NewspaperArchive.** This is a library networked database which has newspaper articles from around the country. You can search Madison's newspapers, which ran features on all of Wright's buildings (especially the later ones – Unitarian, Rudin, and Monona Terrace).
- **Wisconsin Historical Society AHI.**[1] This is the State historic Preservation Office inventory of Historic Buildings.
- **National Park Service.**[2]**/national register/National Historic Landmarks**[3] Most buildings (not Monona Terrace) are listed properties, and have forms about them. Most are downloadable.
- **Interviews.** Interview residents or others knowledgeable about the building! Ask me for contacts.
- **Class Google photos pages for photos.**
- **Getty Images.**[4] Just go nuts here.

---

1. *Wisconsin Historical Society,* http://www.wisconsinhistory.org/Content.aspx?dsNav=N:1189.
2. *National Park Service,* https://www.nps.gov/nr/research/.
3. *National Historic Landmarks,* https://www.nps.gov/nhl/.
4. *Getty Images,* http://www.gettyimages.com/photos/frank-lloyd-wright?sort=mostpopular&excludenudity=true&mediatype=photography&phrase=frank%20llc

- **Historical Society image database.**[5] Full of photos of our buildings. Go nuts here, too.
- **Websites.** Websites discussed early on in class (linked on learn@UW)

You need to come up with a logically flowing, clear narrative. Minimum of the interpretive section is 3-4 paragraphs, but it may be longer. It should – like your contribution to chapter 1 – be abundantly illustrated (use the sources above).

Information on reference format will come later. For now, use parenthetical citations. We will convert them (most likely) to footnotes by the end of term. Make sure to keep a bibliography of your sources.

Groups. I've listed the groups below, but these may change depending on a variety of factors.

Lamp – [student names redacted]

Gilmore – [student names redacted]

PEW – [student names redacted]

Jacobs – [student names redacted]

Rudin – [student names redacted]

Unitarian – [student names redacted]

Monona Terrace – [student names redacted]

The Pressbooks site has been set up with chapters for each group (take a look!).

If you have any questions at any time, please let me know.

---

5. Image Database, *Wisconsin Historical Society*, http://www.wisconsinhistory.org/Content.aspx?dsNav=N:1135.

PART V

RESOURCES

Here are some further resources to help you get started making open textbook projects in your classroom. This is the first edition of this guide. We welcome your feedback and ideas to expand it!

Chapter 17

CC Licensing Guide

ZOE WAKE HYDE

WHAT IS A COPYRIGHT LICENSE?

Copyright restricts the use of creative works (written text, photos, graphics, music, film etc.) to the creator unless they give explicit permission to another person or company to use their work in a particular way — think of an author allowing their book to be made into a film, or an artist allowing their artwork to be printed on a t shirt.

These permissions are called licenses, and the resulting products are called derivative works.

Traditionally, these licenses have been granted on a case-by-case basis, and require every person seeking a license to contact the creator every time, for every use.

WHAT ARE THE CREATIVE COMMONS LICENSES?

Creative Commons (CC) licenses give people "a simple, standardized way to grant copyright permissions to their creative work" (Creative Commons). Instead of requiring each person wanting to use, share or adapt the creative work to ask permission, a CC license allows the creator to indicate upfront what they will and won't allow others to do with their work.

There are several CC licenses, each of which grants different levels of permission to the public. Each of these licenses provides conditions for appropriate use, and can be differently suited to both specific kinds of creative content and the preferences of a work's creator(s).

CC-BY: Attribution

Anyone is free to **share & adapt** the work, as long as they give appropriate credit, provide a link to the license and indicate if changes were made to the original material.

CC-BY-SA: Attribution-Share Alike

Anyone is free to **share & adapt** the work, as long as they give appropriate credit, provide a link to the license, and indicate if changes were made to the original material. **Any derivative works must share the same license as the original material**. This means that if someone remixes your work, or makes a new project that uses your work, they must also license that work under a CC-BY-SA license.

CC-BY-NC: Attribution-Non Commercial

Anyone is free to **share & adapt** the work for any **non-commercial use**, as long as they give appropriate credit, provide a link to the license and indicate if changes were made to the original material.

CC-BY-ND: Attribution-No Derivatives
Anyone is free to **share** the work, as long as they give appropriate credit, provide a link to the license and indicate if changes were made to the original material. **Any derivative works may not be distributed**. This means that you can make a remix or new project that makes use of the original work for private use, but cannot share or publish your derivative work.

CC-BY-NC-SA: Attribution-Non Commercial-Share Alike
Anyone is free to **share & adapt** the work for any **non-commercial use**, as long as they give appropriate credit, provide a link to the license, and indicate if changes were made to the original material. **Any derivative works must share the same license as the original material.**

CC-BY-NC-ND: Attribution-Non Commercial-No Derivatives
Anyone is free to **share** the work for any **non commercial use**, as long as they give appropriate credit, provide a link to the license, and indicate if changes were made to the original material. **Any derivative works may not be distributed.**

These are also referred to as "open" licenses, a category that includes other kinds of licenses used for things like open source software.

WHY ARE CC LICENSES IMPORTANT TO OPEN TEXTBOOKS?

Open licenses are critical to open textbooks because they grant the public, including students and faculty, the right to retain, reuse, revise, remix and redistribute educational content without charge. These rights are referred to as the 5 Rs, and are the foundation for defining what counts as Open Educational Resources (OERs) (Open Content).

First of all, an open license guarantees free (unpaid) access to content for students. With the rising costs of textbooks, student loans, and costs of living, creating and supporting free educational materials is one way faculty and institutions can make a difference for their students.

> An open license guarantees free (unpaid) access to content for students.

While reducing the cost of education is already a big deal, the most permissive CC licenses also allow faculty and students the freedom to adapt content to make it work for them. With the exception of "No Derivatives" licensed work (which is generally not recognised as "open" for educational uses), CC-licensed works can be pulled apart, put back together, changed, updated, localised, translated, re-ordered, re-worked, annotated, expanded, simplified, customised, combined* and turned blue at will.

Without a CC license, any of these uses could be a violation of copyright law.

What this means in practical terms is that textbooks can be adapted to suit the needs of any given course, rather than a course being adapted to a textbook (or only using a handful of chapters out of a $200 textbook). And faculty and universities don't have to worry about the grey areas of copyright law, or the risk of a lawsuit.

Note: different CC licenses may or may not be compatible for combining/remixing. See CC's license compatibility chart for more details.

WHY USE CC-BY SPECIFICALLY?

The CC-BY license is considered the gold standard for open textbooks because it allows the most freedom, and it is the only license that enables all of the 5 Rs without restriction.

> **Share Alike (SA)** can limit remixing potential with content under different licenses
> **No Derivatives (ND)** doesn't allow derivative works, which means no revision or remixing, negating many of the advantages of open textbooks
> **Non Commercial (NC)** can create uncertainty as to what qualifies as a "commercial use" (e.g. selling a printed course pack)

CC-BY lets everyone working with openly licensed educational materials to get the most value, benefit, and use possible from the work we all put in.

WHAT ARE MY RIGHTS WHEN I USE THE CC-BY LICENSE?

If you license your work under a CC-BY license for an open textbook project (or anywhere else!), you retain the copyright, meaning the work is still yours. The license can be thought of as "some rights reserved" rather than "all rights reserved."

1. You have the right to be attributed correctly on all versions of your work, as well as any derivative works, and any changes made to your work are required to be identified.
2. You also have the right to not be attributed on your work or any derivative version of it, if at any stage you decide you don't want to be associated with it.
3. Last, you have the right to change the license applied to your work at any time, BUT this will only apply to future users — anyone already using your work will retain the rights given to them in the original license.

All of these rights come with the caveat that once content is online it can circulate widely and be nearly impossible to trace. This means that practically speaking, while it is easy to remove your name or change the license on the original copy of your work, it is very difficult to do so on any other copies or derivative works. Keep this in mind at the start of your project when selecting a license.

WHAT'S THE BIGGER PICTURE HERE?

Would you like to help us expand this section? Indicate your interest in the Rebus Community Forum.

Chapter 18

MOU for Students and Faculty

ZOE WAKE HYDE

> The following agreement template can be used to clearly lay out the rights of students when participating in a collaborative open textbook project, and the responsibilities of the faculty member to their students. Its purpose is to make sure that students are informed about the requirements of the project and the implications of the license they choose.
>
> Please feel free to adapt it or extend it as you see fit for the purposes of your class, and share any feedback that may improve the template for future uses.

AGREEMENT TO CONTRIBUTE TO OPEN TEXTBOOK

I, _____, agree to participate in the creation of _____, an open textbook, in collaboration with my professor, _____. This work will comprise [part of] my coursework for _____ [class/course name].

I understand that inclusion of my work in the final text is conditional upon my willingness to license my contributions under a CC-BY license.

I have read the Guide to Creative Commons Licenses and understand that a CC-BY license allows others to share, use and adapt my work so long as they attribute me as the original author.

I understand that I have the right to request that my name and/or work be removed from the original text, or change the license on my contributions at any stage prior to publication.

Signed: _____ Date: _____

I, _____, agree to work with my student _____ on the creation of _____, an open textbook in [partial] completion of _____ [class/course name].

I commit to supporting _____ throughout this project, and ensuring they have the knowledge and resources they need to be an informed contributor.

I agree that the student may request that their name and/or work be removed from the original text or change the license on their contributions to this work at any stage prior to publication of the work.

I confirm that the student's decision to change the license they place on their work or to not participate in the project will not impact on their course assessment.

Signed: _____ Date: _____

Chapter 19

Course: Becoming an Open Educator

APURVA ASHOK

Becoming an Open Educator[1] is a great resource for faculty or instructors who are wondering about the benefits and impact of open. It begins with a basic introduction to the tenets of Open Education, and later answers more in-depth questions about creating and disseminating Open Educational Resources. This online course is designed to let you work at your own pace, while also providing you with activities, quizzes, and access to additional resources. You can interact with peers, maintain a reflective log, and earn a badge of completion. This relatively straightforward course was developed as part of the Opening Educational Practices in Scotland (OEPS) and supplies the foundational information required for anyone who is curious about the power of open.

---

1. "Becoming an Open Educator," *OpenLearnCreate*, http://www.open.edu/openlearncreate/course/view.php?id=2274.

ABOUT THE PUBLISHER

A Guide to Making Open Textbooks With Students was produced by the Rebus Community for Open Textbook Creation, an initiative of the Rebus Foundation.

The Rebus Community is developing a new, collaborative process for publishing open textbooks and associated content. Rebus is building tools and resources to support open textbook publishing, and to bring together a community of faculty, librarians, students, and others working with open textbooks around the world.

We want to make it easy for the community to contribute to the creation of open textbooks (their own, or others'), and support the creation of new, high-quality open textbooks, available for free to anyone, in standard formats (web, EPUB, MOBI, PDF, and print).

Would you like to help? Join us in the Rebus Community Forum.[1]

---

1. *Rebus Community Forum*, http://forum.rebus.community/.

LICENSING INFORMATION

This book is licensed CC-BY except where otherwise noted.

This license allows for reuse, adaptation, remixing and redistribution of content, so long as you attribute it to the original author(s), indicate if changes are made, and link to the original, free content, found at https://press.rebus.community/makingopentextbookswithstudents/.

PLEASE CREDIT US AS FOLLOWS:

Redistributing the book verbatim:

This material is created by Elizabeth Mays, Robin DeRosa, Rajiv Jhangjiani, Timothy Robbins, David Squires, Anna Andrzejewski, Julie Ward, Alice Barrett, Samara Burns, Amanda Coolidge, Gabriel Higginbotham, Matthew Moore, Maxwell Nicholson, Steel Wagstaff, Zoe Wake Hyde and Apurva Ashok, and produced with support from the Rebus Community. The original is freely available under the terms of the CC-BY 4.0 license at https://press.rebus.community/makingopentextbookswithstudents/.

Revised or adapted versions:

This material is based on original work by Elizabeth Mays, Robin DeRosa, Rajiv Jhangjiani, Timothy Robbins, David Squires, Anna Andrzejewski, Julie Ward, Alice Barrett, Samara Burns, Amanda Coolidge, Gabriel Higginbotham, Matthew Moore, Maxwell Nicholson, Steel Wagstaff, Zoe Wake Hyde and Apurva Ashok, and produced with support from the Rebus Community. The original is freely available under the terms of the CC-BY 4.0 license at https://press.rebus.community/makingopentextbookswithstudents/.

Individual chapters or pieces:

This material is [created by or based on] original work by [chapter or piece author], and produced with support from the Rebus Community. The original is freely available under the terms of the CC-BY 4.0 license at https://press.rebus.community/makingopentextbookswithstudents/.

OTHER OPEN TEXTBOOKS PRODUCED WITH REBUS COMMUNITY SUPPORT

Financial Strategy for Public Managers[1] (Sharon Kioko and Justin Marlowe): University of Washington professors Sharon Kioko and Justin Marlowe used Pressbooks to create a book for students in Master of Public Administration programs. One of many projects of the Rebus Community, this textbook has been designed to serve as the core text for a comprehensive introductory graduate or advanced undergraduate course on public financial management. Kioko and Marlowe have collaborated with the Rebus Community to use this book as a test-case for accessibility and inclusive design in open textbooks.

Media Innovation & Entrepreneurship[2] (Edited by Michelle Ferrier & Elizabeth Mays): More than 20 authors and numerous reviewers including student beta testers were involved in the making of this open textbook project led by co-editors Michelle Ferrier, a former associate dean at Ohio University and Elizabeth Mays, an adjunct faculty at Arizona State University, with support from the Rebus Community. The editors sought to fill a gap in resources for the growing number of faculty who teach media innovation, journal-

1. https://press.rebus.community/financialstrategy/
2. https://press.rebus.community/media-innovation-and-entrepreneurship/

ism entrepreneurship, and the business of journalism in journalism and mass communications programs.

Literature Reviews for Education & Nursing Graduate Students[3] (Linda Frederiksen, Sue F. Phelps): This book from authors Linda Frederiksen and Sue F. Phelps, librarians at Washington State University, helps students recognize the significant role the literature review plays in the research process and prepare them for the work that goes into writing one. Students learn how to form a research question, search existing literature, synthesize results, and write the review. *Literature Reviews for Education and Nursing Graduate Students* also contains examples, checklists, supplementary materials, and additional resources. It was built with support from Rebus Community.

The Open Anthology of Earlier American Literature[4] (Timothy Robbins, Editor): Timothy Robbins of Graceland University built upon Robin DeRosa's popular *Open Anthology of Earlier American Literature* in this community-built work-in-progress supported by the Rebus Community. "My own 'American Literature to 1900' course charts some of the various, often contentious stories of "American" culture's movements towards inclusion, emancipation, and equality across those four centuries of coverage," he says. "The sections track roughly chronologically and feature representative authors and texts. Indigenous creation stories confront European colonial documents; the early texts of New England's Puritan pulpits are met and challenged by the voices and pens of native peoples, African slaves, and women writers. The American Revolution gives way to an explosion of social movements and

---

3. https://press.rebus.community/literaturereviewsedunursing/
4. https://press.rebus.community/openamlit/

an expansion of the canon stretching from Thomas Paine's republican propaganda to the birth of African-American letters in Phillis Wheatley. The selections from the early nineteenth century include the familiar names of the 'American Renaissance'—Emerson, Poe, Hawthorne, Whitman, Melville—in tandem with the literature of abolitionism. The post-Civil War sections aim to balance the significant social writings of the Gilded Age and Reconstruction era with the emergence of realist fiction."

Blueprint for Success[5] (Dave Dillon): A free, Open Educational Resource, Blueprint for Success in College and Career is a students' guide for classroom and career success. This text, designed to show how to be successful in college and in career preparation, focuses on study skills, time management, career exploration, health, and financial literacy.

The *Blueprint for Success* series comprises three books for the College Success and FYE (First-Year Experience) genre. The central text, Blueprint for Success in College and Career, is designed to show how to be successful in college and in career preparation. In addition, targeted sections on Study Skills and Time Management, and Career and Decision Making are available separately as *Blueprint for Success in College: Indispensable Study Skills and Time Management Strategies*[6], and *Blueprint for Success in Career Decision Making*[7]. All have been peer-reviewed by an experienced team.

---

5. https://press.rebus.community/blueprint2/
6. https://press.rebus.community/blueprint1/
7. https://press.rebus.community/blueprint3/

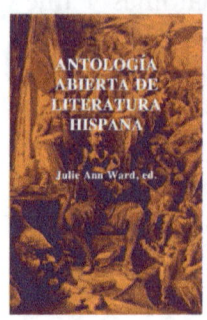
Antología abierta de literatura hispánica[8] (Julie Ann Ward):Una antología crítica de textos literarios del mundo hispanohablante. Se enfoca en autores canónicos y también se intenta incluir voces marginadas. Cada texto tiene una introducción y anotaciones creadas por estudiantes. // A critical anthology of literary texts from the Spanish-speaking world. A focus on canonical authors and an attempt to include voices that have been marginalized. Each text includes an introduction and annotations created by students. You can also contribute to the expansion of this text by having your students contribute! Find out more about implementing the assignment[9].

The Science of Human Nutrition[10] (University of Hawai'i at Mānoa Food Science and Human Nutrition Program): This peer-reviewed textbook serves as an introduction to nutrition for undergraduate students and is the OER textbook for the FSHN 185 The Science of Human Nutrition course at the University of Hawai'i at Mānoa. The book covers basic concepts in human nutrition, key information about essential nutrients, basic nutritional assessment, and nutrition across the lifespan.

---

8. https://press.rebus.community/aalh/
9. https://projects.rebus.community/resource/wtR1EipwAKtTRVpviKmmkZ/expanding-the-anthology
10. http://pressbooks.oer.hawaii.edu/humannutrition/

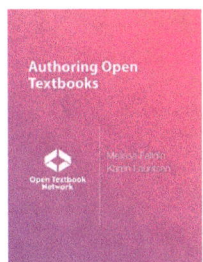*Authoring Open Textbooks*[11] (Melissa Falldin and Karen Lauritsen): This guide is for faculty authors, librarians, project managers and others who are involved in the production of open textbooks in higher education and K-12. Content includes a checklist for getting started, publishing program case studies, textbook organization and elements, writing resources and an overview of useful tools.

If you are planning on adopting or adapting any of these open textbooks, please let us know[12]!

---

11. https://press.rebus.community/authoropen/
12. https://goo.gl/forms/Je9v8V30F3u4hkKg2

AS SEEN IN

The *Guide to Making Open Textbooks With Students* has been seen in:

- **Inside Higher Ed:** "Students' Vital Role in OER,"[1] Christina Hendricks
- **OER Digest:** September 7, 2017[2]
- **Girl Meets Web:** "OER Resources? Start Here!"[3]
- **You're the Teacher:** "Open Pedagogy: Examples of Class Activities: An Upcoming Talk I'm Giving,"[4] Christina Hendricks
- **SlideShare:** "What's Open About Open Pedagogy?"[5] Christina Hendricks
- **Medium:** "Getting Started With Pressbooks,"[6] Steel Wagstaff
- **University of Connecticut:** "Guides to Adapting and Creating OER Textbooks & Learning Materials"[7]
- **University of Guelph:** "Accessible Course Content & Open Educational Resources"[8]

1. https://www.insidehighered.com/digital-learning/views/2017/12/13/students-have-vital-role-creating-and-spreading-oer
2. https://oerdigest.org/2017/09/15/oer-digest-september-7th-2017/
3. http://girlmeetsweb.com/index.php/2016/11/07/oer-resources-start-here/
4. https://blogs.ubc.ca/chendricks/2017/10/08/open-pedagogy-examples/comment-page-1/
5. https://www.slideshare.net/clhendricksbc/whats-open-about-open-pedagogy-final-version
6. https://medium.com/@steelwagstaff/getting-started-with-pressbooks-ee3e5f07f4d2
7. https://open.uconn.edu/tools-create/

- **The University of Arizona:** "OER 101"[9]
- **Austin Community College District:** "Open Educational Resources: Open Pedagogy Examples"[10]
- **University of Arkansas:** "Information and Links for Open Education and Open Educational Resources,"[11]
- **University of Nevada, Reno:** "Open Educational Resources: How to Author"[12]
- **BYU Library:** "Affordable Course Materials: Open Educational Resources"[13]
- **Gamification and OER Promotion:** Gamification and OER Promotion[14]
- **Georgia State University:** "Open Education: For Educators and Open Textbook Authors"[15]
- **Australian Catholic University:** "Finding Open Access Resources"[16]
- **Washington University in St. Louis:** "Open Access Textbooks"[17]
- **Teaching in Higher Ed:** "Question from a Listener: Open Textbooks,"[18] Bonni Stachowiak

8. https://www.lib.uoguelph.ca/find/find-type-resource/accessible-course-content-open-educational-resources
9. https://webcache.googleusercontent.com/search?q=cache:y-82coDyw9MJ:oer.arizona.edu/sites/oer.sites.arizona.edu/files/OER%2520101%2520handout_AzLA%25202017.doc+&cd=20&hl=en&ct=clnk&gl=us
10. http://researchguides.austincc.edu/oer/openpedexamples
11. https://uark.libguides.com/c.php?g=391653&p=2812202
12. https://guides.library.unr.edu/oer/create
13. http://guides.lib.byu.edu/c.php?g=300037&p=2004063
14. https://services.bridgew.edu/bscannounce/uploads/Gamification%20and%20OER%20Promotion.pdf
15. http://research.library.gsu.edu/c.php?g=115771&p=752918
16. https://libguides.acu.edu.au/findingopenaccessresources/OER
17. http://libguides.wustl.edu/ebooks/opentextbooks
18. http://teachinginhighered.com/2018/01/21/question-from-a-listener-open-textbooks/

- **Wikiversity:** Open Educational Resources Lesson[19]
- **Open Pedagogy on the Open Lab:** "Open Pedagogy Event: Teaching and Learning with Annotation,"[20] Kristen Hackett
- **Open Up: Conversations on Open Education for Language Learning:** "Student Authored Textbooks… in the Language Classroom?"[21]

---

19. https://en.wikiversity.org/wiki/Open_Educational_Resources/Lesson
20. https://openlab.citytech.cuny.edu/openpedagogyopenlab/2017/10/19/open-pedagogy-event-th-1026-teaching-and-learning-with-annotation/
21. http://blog.coerll.utexas.edu/student-authored-textbooks-in-the-language-classroom/

www.ingramcontent.com/pod-product-compliance
Lightning Source LLC
LaVergne TN
LVHW020138080526
838202LV00048B/3971